Significant Harm: its management and outcome

Edited by
Margaret Adcock
Richard White
&
Anne Hollows

First published 1991
by Significant Publications
42 High Street
Croydon CR0 1YB

ISBN 0 9518761 0 4

Design and Production by Lasso 071 272 9141
Print by Greenshires

Contributors

Margaret Adcock is a social work consultant, teacher and guardian ad litem.

Arnon Bentovim is consultant child psychiatrist at Great Ormond Street Hospital and the Tavistock Clinic, London.

Hamish Cameron is consultant child psychiatrist at St George's Hospital, London.

David Jones is consultant child psychiatrist at the Park Hospital, Oxford.

Annie Lau is consultant child and family psychiatrist at the Child and Family Consultation Centre, Ilford, Essex.

Margaret Lynch is senior lecturer in community paediatrics at Guys Hospital, London.

Tony Morrison is a social work consultant and teacher.

John Simmonds is senior lecturer in social work at Goldsmith's College, London University.

Richard White is a solicitor and writer on family law.

Stephen Wolkind is consultant child psychiatrist at the Maudsley Hospital, London.

Eileen Vizard is consultant child psychiatrist at the Tavistock Clinic, London.

Contents

Introduction

Stephen Wolkind

This book could be seen as the first attempt by a group of professionals to debate significant harm and its implications. All the contributors met with others in September 1990 to develop the thinking on significant harm for a paper to be included in the Child Protection Training Pack, published by the National Children's Bureau as part of the Department of Health's Children Act training initiative. Since then further discussion and study of recent research and of Guidance material, produced in conjunction with the Act's implementation, has resulted in the development of these papers which consider the definition, assessment and treatment of significant harm from a multi-disciplinary perspective.

At the time of the original meeting, training and teaching about the Children Act 1989 was well underway. One of these papers, that by Jones and his child psychiatric colleagues, is based upon a handout given to participants in the Judicial Studies Board series of teaching events. These sessions show well the remarkable effect the Act is having. For the first time judges from both the county courts and the High Court, and magistrates, were brought together to hear from and discuss with professionals from a wide range of disciplines. Normally they would meet only within the formality of the court. If the Act achieves nothing else, it has caused a major breakthrough in getting the different professionals working within child care law to understand the techniques, constraints, ideas and values underpinning each other's work.

Most of the teaching courses have been designed to get over the basic principles behind the Act, the procedures which need to be followed and the new powers of the court. This publication is, however, rather different. Section 31(2) of the Act requires the court to be satisfied as to the occurrence of significant harm, or the likelihood of it, and its causes, before making a care or supervision order. The courts will have a major task in defining what is meant by this term and what are its limits. In this book, a group of professionals begin to debate what this term might mean

1

to them and how they would seek to define it to the courts.

White analyses the actual wording and considers how the legal criteria might work in practice. Adcock takes a practical approach, looking at what social services departments might actually be able to do and identifying some of the tensions for both practitioners and the families with whom they work. Bentovim provides a psychiatric account of significant harm, looking in particular at the potential long term effects of different forms of abuse; an approach which will underline much medical evidence in court. Jones looks at the importance of seeing how long term effects of abuse may be modified by intervention while Morrison considers the need for intervention to be underpinned by the use of court orders. The Act pays great attention to children's ethnic and cultural identity and needs and these are addressed by Lau, a child psychiatrist of Chinese ethnic origin. Jones et al describe the process by which psychiatrists assess and determine the evidence which they will present to court. Lynch looks at similar issues from a paediatric perspective. In conclusion, Simmonds provides a view from academic social work. It is exciting to see how he has borrowed concepts such as sensitivity and specificity from orthodox epidemiology and demonstrated how they can be applied to child care work.

This is obviously not a comprehensive guide to the meaning of significant harm. It is, however, the first step towards reaching a consensus as to what it actually means. It is to be hoped that before long a follow up will be provided describing how the courts are defining in legal terms a notion which to many might still seem vague and potentially hard to delineate, as well as addressing the practical consequences for professionals. Meanwhile, this book will be deemed a success if it encourages inter-disciplinary discussion throughout the country on Significant Harm and most importantly, how it can be identified, treated or better still prevented.

Examining the threshold criteria

Richard White

Introduction

Section 31 of the Children Act 1989 requires the court to be satisfied, before making a care or supervision order and before applying the principles in section 1 of the Act, that certain criteria (referred to as the 'threshold criteria') exist. The chart at figure 1 illustrates the matters to be considered.

Even though the threshold criteria are satisfied the court may still decide not to make a care or supervision order. It has to consider the checklist in section 1(3) and in particular (g), the range of orders available to the court, which include the orders under section 8 of the Act. Those orders can be made whether or not the threshold criteria are satisfied.

Harm

The central concept of the criteria is harm. It is defined by section 31(9) to mean ill-treatment or the impairment of health or development. There is no question of needing to satisfy more than one of these conditions; they are to be regarded as alternatives. In relation to the similar words used in the Children and Young Persons Act 1969, Lord Brandon said in D (a minor) v Berkshire County Council [1987] 1 ALL ER 20: "So to regard them is in no way inconsistent with the likelihood that, in many cases, any two of the three situations, or indeed all three of them, may co-exist". Under the previous legislation it has also been held that rules as to duplicity do not apply in care proceedings: Wooley v Haines (1975) 140 JP 16.

Ill treatment

Ill-treatment is defined as including sexual abuse and forms of ill-

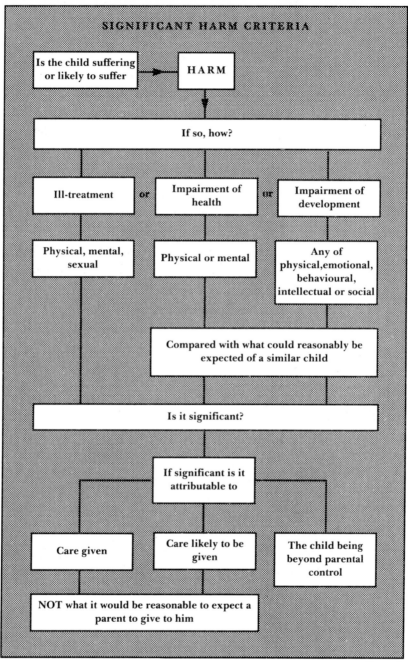

figure 1

treatment which are not physical: s31(9). It must by implication include physical abuse. The inclusion of emotional abuse gives statutory effect to the decision in F v Suffolk County Council (*1981*) 2FLR 208.

Ill-treatment is sufficient in itself and it is not necessary to show, in order to satisfy the criteria, that impairment of health or development has followed, or is likely to follow, as a consequence, although that might be relevant to the question of whether the court should make an order.

Where ill-treatment is alleged the court may wish to try to identify the person(s) responsible for the ill-treatment in view of the need to attribute harm to parental care or the failure to prevent harm. It will be a matter for judicial interpretation as to whether the test to be applied to the ill-treatment and identification of the person responsible will be the balance of probabilities or the higher test applied when identifying an individual in sexual abuse cases in Re W (minors) (*Child Abuse: Evidence*) [*1987*] 1FLR 397.

Health or development

Impairment of health or development can also provide the basis of the harm. Health is further defined as physical or mental health and development as physical, intellectual, emotional or behavioural development: s31(9).

Comparison with 'similar child'

Where the facts relate to health or development it is also necessary to compare the health or development with what could reasonably be expected of a similar child: s31(10). This raises questions about interpretation of a 'similar child' on which the courts will have to pronounce. Is it a child from the same neighbourhood? Should the courts be applying different standards to children from different ethnic backgrounds? Should the courts compare a child who has learning difficulties with another child who has similar difficulties? What if those difficulties are caused by parental care?

Department of Health Guidance Volume 1 'Court Orders' states: "The meaning of 'similar' in this context will require judicial interpretation, but may need to take account of environmental, social and cultural characteristics of the child. The need to use a standard appropriate for the child arises because some children have characteristics or handicaps which mean that they cannot be expected to be as healthy or well-developed as others. Equally if the child needs special care or attention (because, for example, he is unusually difficult to control) then this is to be expected for him. The standard should only be that which it is reasonable to expect for the particular child, rather than the best that could possibly be achieved; applying a 'best' standard could open up the risk that a child might be removed from home simply because some other arrangements could cater better for his needs than care by his parents." (*para 3.20*)

(For further discussion of this issue see 'Care after 1991': M. Freeman in 'Children and the Law' (*1990, ed Freestone*), and 'Care after 1991 – a reply': A. Bainham in the 'Journal of Child Law' (*1991 p99*).)

Is the harm significant?

Whatever the nature of the harm, the court has to consider whether the harm caused is in itself significant. The word is not defined in the Act: a common sense definition should be applied. 'Significant' is defined by the Oxford English Dictionary as considerable, noteworthy or important, "Minor shortcomings in health care or minor deficits in physical, psychological or social development should not require compulsory intervention unless cumulatively they are having, or are likely to have, serious and lasting effects upon the child." (*Guidance 'Court Orders' para 3.21*) These are clearly matters of fact for the court, but it would appear that the significance could relate to the seriousness of the harm or the implications of it. For example, a broken leg would be a serious injury, but the implications of a small cigarette burn might be greater.

Is the child suffering or likely to suffer harm?

The court must also consider whether the child is suffering harm currently or whether he is likely to suffer it. The threshold criteria may not be satisfied on the basis of an isolated incident from which the child has recovered, unless it is such as to suggest that the child is likely to suffer in the future. The existence of past harm is not in itself sufficient to satisfy the criteria, although it may be relevant to the question of whether harm is likely to be suffered.

The case of M v Westminster City Council [1985] FLR 93 would appear to have continuing relevance in the interpretation of whether the child is suffering harm. There it was held, in relation to care proceedings under the Children and Young Persons Act 1969, that the court was not restricted to considering whether the child's development was being prevented at the time of hearing. Butler Sloss J (as she then was) said: "A child's development is a continuing process. The present must be relevant in the context of what has happened in the past and it becomes a matter of how far in the past you go." This approach was approved by the House of Lords in D v Berkshire County Council [1987] AC 317. It will also enable the court to consider, in the case of a child suffering harm, whether the threshold criteria were satisfied when the proceedings were started, since by the time of the hearing the harm may have been abated by removal from the source of harm.

Department of Health Guidance (para 3.22) suggests that the 'likely to suffer' clause allows proceedings to be considered where, for example, the child had suffered significant harm in the past and is likely to do so again because of some recurring circumstance, such as abuse associated with bouts of parental depression; or where a newly-born baby, because of the family history, would be at risk if taken home; or where the welfare of a child being looked after in local authority accommodation would be at risk if the parents went ahead with plans to return him to an unsuitable home environment.

Judicial interpretation may also be necessary for the question of what is 'likely'. It could be argued that 'likely' means 'probable', which suggests a standard perhaps as high as a 75% test; or 'more likely than not', that is, on the balance of probabilities. Perhaps the preferred test should be that the harm is higher than a mere possibility but not as high as 'more likely that not', about a one in three possibility. This interpretation would enable the court to be satisfied as to the threshold criteria, so that it could then consider the other tests in section 1. It remains to be seen whether the court will take into account the possible serious effect of harm even though the likelihood of its occurrence is lower.

Is the harm attributable to care given or likely to be given?

Having satisfied itself that the harm is significant, the court has also to be satisfied that it is attributable to the care given, or likely to be given, to the child not being what a parent would give to the child. The likely care complements the likely harm. Harm caused solely by a third party is therefore excluded, unless the parent has failed to prevent it.

If the child is being accommodated at the time of the proceedings, the test to be applied would be in relation to the care that was likely to be given to the child without the making of the order. If the case relates to harm likely to be suffered, this could relate to the inadequate care actually being given, or to the possible deterioration of barely adequate care, or the care likely to be given if the parent resumed care. This part of the provision must also cover those cases where the child is being accommodated and the local authority wants to make plans for the child with which the parent does not agree. If the lack of security of the child in the placement is causing the child to suffer significant harm, and the parent is not going to resume care, the authority may wish to seek an order so as to make suitable arrangements.

Care is not defined in the Act, but it must be more than the mere physical care that would be provided if the parent were to resume care of the child. It should connote love and attention, without which it could be argued that the child will suffer harm even though not returned home. The court will have to consider the plans of the parent and how the parent has exercised parental responsibility in the past. In this context, any agreements which have been reached, what the parents have been told about the importance of acting in accordance with them and the extent to which they have been carried out or otherwise will be relevant factors. The question of degree is a matter of fact for the court, but a failure to exercise parental responsibility must provide some evidence that the threshold criteria are satisfied.

If any harm suffered by an accommodated child would result from the move, rather than the care likely to be given, the criteria may not be satisfied.

Care of the reasonable parent

Section 31 specifies that the care must be not 'what it would be reasonable to expect a parent to give'. This requires a test to be applied as to what a hypothetical reasonable parent would provide, so that parents cannot argue that they have particular problems, that they are feckless, unintelligent, irresponsible, alcoholic, drug abusers, poor, or otherwise disadvantaged, justifying them in providing a lower standard of care. Those matters might be relevant to the question of whether an order should be made, if their problems could be ameliorated by the provision of other services by the local authority. They will not, however enable them to avoid fulfilling the threshold criteria. Guidance suggests that the court will wish to see professional evidence on the standards of care which reasonable parents could be expected to provide, with support from community wide services as appropriate where the child's needs are complex or demanding, or where the lack of reasonable care is not immediately obvious (*para 3.23*).

Care of the child in question

This section also provides for 'a parent to give to *him*'. Thus it is the child in question, rather than an average child, whose parenting needs must be considered. If the child has particular difficulties, say in relation to his behaviour or handicap, the court will have to consider what a reasonable parent would provide for him. This could require a higher standard of care than for an average child.

Application of section 1 principles

Having satisfied itself as to the threshold criteria, the court must then regard the welfare of the child as the paramount consideration (s1(3)). It must also consider the checklist contained in section 1(3).

Even though the threshold criteria are satisfied, the court may still decide not to make a care or supervision order. Clause (g) of the checklist in section 1(3) requires the court to consider the range of orders available to the court, which includes orders under section 8 of the Act. Since proceedings under s31 are 'family proceedings' (s8(4)), s8 orders can be made whether or not the threshold criteria are satisfied, and whether or not any party makes an application (s10(1)). The court could consider making a conditional residence order in favour of a parent, or a residence order in favour of a third party such as a relative or foster parent. Additional s8 orders, for example relating to contact, could be made in support of a plan for the child.

The court must also consider whether it is better for the child to make an order than to make no order at all (s1(5)). In the context of care proceedings this will mean that the court will have to consider the plans which the authority is proposing for the child, whatever order is made. Are they the best plans available for the child, and if so, why is an order, whether under s8 or s31, necessary to those plans. The degree of detail of any plans which will be required by the court is a matter for debate but it should be noted that the application form prescribed by the Rules of Court for a care or supervision order requires the applicant to state the plans for the child.

The court cannot require the local authority to provide services under Part III of the Act. It must, however, consider whether the provision of services, either in support of the child remaining at home or, with the parents' agreement, to accommodate the child, would provide an alternative which would promote the child's welfare.

Significant harm: implications for the exercise of statutory responsibilities

Margaret Adcock

The Children Act 1989 envisages a tremendous change in the thinking and practice about services to families and about child protection. It is important to remember that this change reflects considerable concern and dissatisfaction about the services that have been offered in the past. The events in Cleveland, the deaths of children including Jasmine Beckford, Kimberley Carlile and Doreen Aston, and the research findings about what has happened to many children in care gave rise to considerable concern and dissatisfaction about the services and remedies being offered to children and families in difficulty. The research made it clear that childrens' attachment needs were not being met, that they were losing touch with their families, that their medical needs were not being attended to, and that some of them were actually being abused in care.

Rupert Hughes, from the Department of Health, said recently that looking back he believed two major underlying themes were identified as needing correction:

- the unsatisfactory nature of the process within the juvenile court which had been designed for purposes other than care proceedings:

- the dominance of a rescue approach to care over a preventive or respite approach which maintained family relationships when possible.

There was a consensus that a new approach to meeting the needs of children was necessary. It was felt that the family was the best place for most children to be raised, and parents rather than local authorities should exercise responsibility for their children and decide what was best for them. To ensure that this happened, certain basic principles should be embodied in the new Act:

- services must be provided to assist certain parents whose children are in need. The local authority must work in partnership with parents and assist them to meet their responsibilities;

- there must be a minimum level of intrusion into family life and therefore the grounds for intervention are more specific;

- the possibility of some parents harming their children is recognised and the duty to investigate this is strengthened;

- at all stages in the course of child protection work, even if significant harm is established, consideration must be given to whether it is possible to work with a voluntary arrangement;

- courts are enjoined not to make an order unless doing so would be better for the child, and to make the least intrusive order necessary;

- if a care order is made, local authorities have a duty to return children to their families wherever possible.

In order to implement these principles, local authorities now have to provide two kinds of service under the Children Act – first for children in need and their families and secondly a child protection service if the question of significant harm arises.

Social workers are likely to rely very greatly on the health services to assist them with definitions of significant harm, of what constitutes abuse and of what is normal development and what is impairment. They are also likely to turn to the education services to define what constitutes a 'similar child' over the age of five. It is vital, however, that social workers seek to form their own definitions in relation to their particular role and functions under the new Act. This is particularly important because there will not in future be an automatic link between the seriousness of any harm and the need for an order as there has often been in the past.

Social work definitions of significant harm must be formulated within the context of the whole Act and the services which may be made available.

However social workers and others must assess the harm and its consequences for the child properly before they make decisions about what should happen next. The significance of the significant harm for the child's future will need to be considered in the light of the parent's recognition of the need to change, their willingness to cooperate in any plan and their ability to do so, as well as the many other factors discussed elsewhere in this book.

It will also be important to distinguish between the components of the abuse itself which cause harm to the child and the harm derived from the response of professionals. Jones (*1991*) points out that it can be difficult to distinguish what is truly iatrogenic (system abuse) from the natural harm and the discovery of the harm itself. For example in the case of intra-familial sexual abuse, it is the discovery itself which is traumatic and disruptive, and in a very real sense the family can never be the same again.

Since local authorities want to prevent harm they need to know how they may unwittingly cause it. Jones lists various examples of such harm, including

over zealous professional intervention;

repeated multiple interviewing or examination;

decision making based on defensiveness;

attendance of the child at court;

placements.

Perhaps the major way in which local authorities may cause harm is by ignoring the importance of attachments and attachment theory. Kagan and Schlosberg (*1989*) have suggested that every plan for children should be scrutinised to see how it meets their attachment needs. Providing a child with attachment in one placement does not mean that the child can subsequently be moved without harm, nor that multiple placements may not have a long term effect. The research findings make a link between numbers of placement and difficulties in both rehabilitation and the placement of children in permanent alternative care (*Martin, 1976; Farmer and Parker, 1991; Rushton, Treseder and Quinton, 1988*). Rowe

(*1991*) points out that little is known about what proportion of those children currently re-admitted to care are able to return to the same placement as before. Nor is there yet any substantive body of research on the effect of multiple separations for the purpose of respite. She warns that in the light of the Act's emphasis on the provision of accommodation as a means of preserving families under stress, this is clearly a serious gap in our knowledge.

Provision of services

The criteria for both preventive and protective services centre on concern about the child's health and development. Both kinds of service are intended to assist families where the development of the children is, or is likely to be, impaired. Both s17, which sets out the duties of local authorities to families of children in need, and s31 which defines the criteria for care proceedings refer to the impairment of health or development as the basic condition which must occur or be likely to occur. In s17, a child is defined as being in need if their health or development is likely to be significantly impaired, or further impaired, without the provision for them of services, or they are disabled. In s31, a court may make a care order if it is satisfied that the child is suffering, or is likely to suffer, significant harm. Harm is defined as ill treatment or the impairment of health or development. This impairment must also be attributable to unreasonable parental care.

The concept of local authority services directed at promoting the healthy development of a child in partnership with parents either within the family or by looking after the child away from the family, on a planned basis, for short or longer periods is new. It moves away from the present duties of local authorities to provide services to prevent the child coming into or remaining in care and to investigate whether there are grounds for care proceedings. These duties have often meant either that local authorities have directed considerable attention to keeping children out of care until a crisis has been reached or if there appear to be grounds for care proceedings they have focused almost entirely on the investigation of child abuse and the need to protect children from the abuser. Services have often been based on global goals rather than individual need.

Neither the organisation of these services nor the evaluation of their effectiveness has usually focused on the wellbeing or individual outcome for the child, as Jones points out in a later chapter. In the USA, for example, there have been strenuous efforts to develop services to prevent children being removed from their parents. Wells and Biegel (*1991*) who studied the evaluation of these placement prevention services found that there was often no differentiation between child placements that were in the interests of children and those that should have been prevented.

The organisation of both preventive and protective services around a central concern for the child's health and development should give local authorities both the opportunity to provide a consistent unified service which meets children's individual needs and criteria for evaluating the services.* It should provide a framework for working on a voluntary basis in some situations even where there is significant harm. However, local authority managers as well as social workers will need to understand child development and the effect of harm on this. The significance of harm cannot be understood without an understanding of development and development cannot be promoted without an understanding of what it is that needs to be promoted.

It will be essential therefore to look in detail at the effect on a child and his family of a particular service and the way in which it is provided. For example accommodating a child on a short term basis from time to time, might well give his parents some respite and fulfil the long term aim of enabling the child to remain in the family. The effect of such placements on the child and his development, however, will be related to his age, whether he has developed secure attachments or is an unattached child, whether he has experienced many previous separations, and whether he is going to a familiar person.

Partnership

The concept of partnership is described in the Department of Health Guidance (*vol 3 para 2*) and is implicit in the Act. The Guidance stresses

*Researchers have devised a comprehensive system of measurement which could monitor the development of all children for whom local authorities take responsibility (*British Journal of Social Work, 1991*).

the need for partnership with parents and consultation with children as a guiding principle for the provisions of services. Working in partnership is not synonymous with working with families on a voluntary basis. It also applies where there is a care order. It is clearly important therefore, for the successful working of the Act that there is a more detailed under-standing, shared by families and professionals, of what is meant by part-nership. Without this neither children nor parents can be offered appropriate safeguards and social workers and members of other disci-plines will not be able to resolve their dual responsibilities for supporting families and protecting children from significant harm.

Partnership derives from the concept of parental responsibility which replaces parental rights and duties. Lord McKay, the Lord Chancellor said in introducing the Children Bill in the House of Lords, that parental responsibility emphasised that the days when a child should be regarded as the possession of his parents were now buried forever. The over-riding purpose of parenthood is the responsibility of caring for and raising the child to be a properly developed adult, both physically and morally.

A parent has responsibility by virtue of Section 2 of the Act. No other person including the local authority, has responsibility for the child or authority to exercise any power over the child without the consent of the parent or a legal mandate ordered by the court, for example the making of a residence order. Anyone offering services to the family must there-fore work in conjunction with the parents. Where a child has sufficient understanding to participate, he/she should also be involved. Since the court shall not make an order unless doing so would be better for the child, the Guidance envisages that in most cases it will be possible to work in partnership with families on a voluntary basis.

Where the court makes an order placing the child in the care of the local authority, the local authority acquires parental responsibility. Section 2(6) provides that a parent who has parental responsibility shall not cease to have that responsibility solely because some other person subsequently acquires parental responsibility for the child. 'Person' in this context includes the local authority, so that they and the parent must continue to work together.

This is limited only if a child is in care by s33(3) which gives the authority power to determine the extent to which a parent or guardian of the child may meet his parental responsibility, if they are satisfied that it is necessary to do so in order to safeguard and promote the welfare of the child.

The meaning of partnership

The dictionary defines partnership as "state of being a partner, sharing, joint business". In the guidance and regulations partnership is perceived in relation to child centred goals. It is not an open ended arrangement. It should be built on a plan arising from an assessment of the child's needs. This is the 'joint business' of partnership. It will be very important that the principle of working in partnership does not become an end in itself but is always related to the needs of the child. Child centred partnership is an appropriate feature of services which are directed at promoting the healthy development of children.

Partnership on a voluntary basis

In considering the need for voluntary services for a child, local authorities must make an assessment. They must assess the existing strengths and skills of the families concerned and help them overcome identified difficulties and enhance strengths. The outcome of any service provision under this power should be evaluated to see whether it has met the primary objective, namely to safeguard or promote the child's welfare.

The Act intends accommodation (s20) to be provided as a service under voluntary arrangements which parents of a child in need may seek to take up so long as it is in the best interests of the child. When offering accommodation or a high level of other services, the local authority must work together with children and their families and draw up a plan which should identify how long the service may be required, what the objective should be, and what else others are expected to do. The Guidance states that the Act presumes a high degree of cooperation between parents and local authorities in negotiating and agreeing what form of accommodation can be offered and the use to be made of it.

Partnership where the child is thought to be at risk of significant harm

In this situation partnership is circumscribed by the local authority's duty to investigate and protect the child. Morrison (*1990*) describes it thus: "the care of children should be based on a partnership between the duties of both the state and parents to protect children from harm." If the parent is unwilling or unable to cooperate with the local authority, when the latter has sought to involve them in protecting the child, the local authority then has to seek the authority of the court to intervene. One of the tests for the new legislation will be whether s31 (the grounds for care proceedings) will achieve this goal.

Partnership where there is a Care Order

The local authority should still try to work in partnership to assess the child's needs and reach an agreement on a plan wherever possible, provided this does not jeopardise the child's welfare. The aim of planning should be to prevent drift, which is not conducive to the child's healthy development, and to help focus the work with the child and family.

Partnership will be achieved by a high level of consultation, and consideration of the views of children, parents and other important people in the child's life at every stage of decision making and review. This is required by s22, when the local authority is looking after, or preparing to look after a child.

Limitations on partnership

Child protection duties may place constraints on some aspects of partnership. Child abuse and neglect reflects an inherent conflict of interest between family members, even if this is only temporary. There are always likely to be some parents who are unable or unwilling to engage in trying to provide more adequately or safely for their children. There will also be some cases where the local authority fears that disclosure of their suspicions might result in threats to the child or the non abusing parent, or to the disposal of evidence or give warning to other adults who may be involved.

The Arrangements for the Placement of Children Regulations 1991 (*Regulations & Guidance Vol 3*) says that how far parents' views will influence decisions and outcomes will depend on the circumstances of the individual case. Paramount attention must be given to the welfare of the child and in cases where it becomes necessary to take child protection measures, that action must override other considerations.

Implications for changes in practice

The consequence of the new legal provisions is that there is now a simultaneous emphasis on partnership with parents, support to families and strong child protection with a minimum reliance on court orders. This is an exciting combination but it is also untried and untested. At this stage there are a number of unpredictable factors which are likely to influence outcome. Examples are community and family attitudes to parental responsibility, the point at which courts will decide that it is in the interests of the child to make an order, the level of resources available to underpin a programme of treatment on a voluntary basis, the professional skill available and necessary to help families change on a voluntary basis, and perhaps most important, how many families can, given optimum levels of available professional resources, change with or without the framework of a court order. It will be essential that there is adequate tracking of the effects of these factors to ensure that children really do benefit.

In the meanwhile there are a number of issues that need to be considered. First, local authorities will have to learn how to work in partnership with parents in both voluntary and compulsory situations and to move between the two where necessary. Although, as already stated, there will be some common features of partnership, whatever the legal status of the child, there will also be some important differences. Where there is no significant harm, the parents are free to choose whether or not they want the services. If there is a court order, the local authority should seek to involve parents in making a plan for the child but they will have certain sanctions if the parents fail to cooperate, eg not returning the child. Where there is no court order but significant harm has been established or continues to be a possibility or a suspicion, the local authority will need to make this clear to parents, seek to involve them in agreeing to a plan to diminish the harm and spell out the consequences if this does not happen. The parents in this voluntary situation would seem to have less freedom than in the first one and the meaning of partnership may be much harder for both families and professionals to define.

There is clearly an inherent tension for both families and local authorities in the concept of partnership when the local authority has to provide them with assistance and services in partnership, but may also have to provide protection for their child. Families will have to know what services are being offered and what powers are being exercised at any given point. Local authorities will have to decide in a particular situation what kind of service to provide. Where there is a suspicion of, or the incidence of significant harm, the following questions must be asked:

- what is the degree of impairment in the child's health or development? Should this trigger the provision of services for a child in need or a statutory investigation? If there is reasonable cause to suspect significant harm, the local authority has a duty to make a statutory investigation (s47) even though it may not be clear whether the harm appears attributable to parental care

- if there is significant harm, can the child be protected on a voluntary basis, as the statutory guidance suggests should be possible in most cases, or should an order be sought?

- should an application be made to the court for an order under Part 5 to continue investigation and/or remove the child, or for a care order at least on an interim basis?

- if parents are unwilling or unable to exercise their parental responsibility to assist in the protection of the child, what is the most effective way for the local authority to provide protection and promote the child's healthy development?

- what is the best way of working in partnership in any of these situations?

Assessment

Good assessment is the foundation for all planning and decision making. (*See the Care of Children – Principles and Practice in Regulations and Guidance, 1990*) It will assume crucial importance under the Act because it will be the basis for answering the questions set out above.

In some cases a decision about emergency proceedings, an application for a child assessment order or for care proceedings will have to be made before a comprehensive assessment has been done. This decision will be based on an identification of harm or suspected harm and the degree of risk to the child if action is not taken to stop the harm. The decision will also involve consideration of why statutory intervention rather than voluntary co-operation is necessary and this is likely to require evidence and some degree of assessment of parental history and attitudes. (*See later chapter by Morrison.*)

If a comprehensive assessment is made at the time of a request for accommodation or services for a child in need, or following expressions of strong concern from other professionals, a good deal of information will already be available when decisions have to be made about emergency proceedings or applications for care proceedings. This should help social workers to work within the new timetable to avoid unnecessary delay. It would mean, however, that it would be desirable to do a comprehensive assessment at a much earlier stage of involvement with a family than often happens at present, for example when the name of a child is placed on the child protection register.

The DoH Guide, Protecting Children, (*1988*) sets out the areas that need to be covered in a comprehensive assessment. The information gathered should then enable the following questions to be answered;

- What is the nature of the actual, or suspected, significant harm or impairment of health or development (if any) in the child? How does this fit into a comprehensive assessment of the child (*see Jones, et al*) for example what are thought to be the effects of the harm on overall functioning and development?

- How serious is the harm thought to be and what will happen in both the short and the long term if it continues?

- What is the evidence of the harm and how firm is it? Where does the evidence come from? The Guidelines on Working Together (*DoH, 1991*) suggest that there must be more than one source of evidence.

- What is the evidence of the degree of risk? Is it sufficient to justify emergency action and/or allow child protection measures to override other considerations such as working in partnership with parents? In deciding how to proceed in such cases social workers should ask themselves whether they need to depart from a voluntary basis and whether other people would support such a decision. If it is thought that courts or other professionals might not agree, careful consideration should be given to the reasons for this. Would more evidence or more discussion or an alternative approach achieve more consensus and still protect the child?

- How is the harm thought to occur? This should encompass if possible both a description and an explanation of what happens. The explanation should try and link observation about the problem with both meaningful past events and the current functioning of individuals, and family interactions. It would therefore take into account all areas of the assessment eg the characteristics, attitudes, behaviour and relationships of both adults and children, their past history and how this is thought to affect present functioning, the adult's view of this child and of any other children, and any recent significant events eg death of an important person, unemployment of a parent, expulsion of a child from school.

- If there is significant harm, how can it be stopped or alleviated? This must mean either helping the parents to change, or if this is not possible, providing the child with a safe place to live that also meets his developmental and attachment needs. Children will be unprotected and at risk of serious harm if there is an automatic assumption that a voluntary approach will be helpful in every case. The decision to proceed on a voluntary basis or seek a court order must therefore be linked with a detailed assessment of parents/carers.

- The research shows clearly that not all parents can be helped to change and that in some cases compulsion may be a necessary basis for change. Who can be helped to change and how this can be done, is discussed in detail in the chapters by Jones and Morrison.

- How should the checklist in s1(3) be used if the case goes to court? It would seem that some of the items in s1 will be considered initially in relation to proving significant harm, eg the child's needs, any harm which he has suffered or is at risk of suffering and parental capacity to meet the child's needs. The list will need to be considered again in relation to the different question of whether an order would be better for the child than not making an order. This will involve consideration of both the need and the prognosis for change and what would be required to achieve this. A possible sequence for considering the checklist would be:

1. Define the child's present and future needs in the light of past significant harm, normal child development and racial, cultural and any other specific considerations.

2. Identify the child's wishes and feelings.

3. Define the changes required to meet the child's future needs, taking into account his wishes and feelings.

4. Assess parental capacity to do this and conditions required to achieve any change.

5. Consider the effects, both positive and negative, on the child of any change and identify the least detrimental alternative.

6. Consider whether any changes can be achieved without an order. If not, make an appropriate recommendation for an order.

Evaluating the information gained in an assessment requires knowledge of the relevant literature, skill, experience of other cases, and an impartial approach. Understanding the implications of a child's racial or cultural needs or a handicap, weighing up alternatives, balancing different kinds of harm and deciding what is the least detrimental alternative for the child imposes further requirements. Social workers who have worked very closely with a family on a comprehensive assessment may have become attached to them and find it difficult to accept the distress or rage that may result from a particular decision. The Care of Children – Principles and Practice in Regulations and Guidance recommends that decisions should be made by a small group consisting mainly of people with direct involvement in the case but including at least one person who is knowledgable but detached and objective. Legal advisers should also be consulted.

The use of statutory authority

"All professionals need to be comfortable with and able to use authority appropriately" (*Working Together*) in order to be able to help families to change and to protect children. This means that local authorities have to explain both protection and partnership aims to families in a way that can be understood by people from different races, cultures and religions. Authority may be derived from professional expertise and or from statutory power. Individual workers are likely to feel more comfortable using authority if they have good supervision, with opportunities to review their work, discuss future options and improve their knowledge base. Workers will need to be able to discuss with families what needs to be done and why. The evidence from research (*Sainsbury*) suggests that families can understand and accept the need for statutory authority if it is exercised in an open and honest way.

Rooney (*1988*) suggests that the better informed the client is concerning what will occur during treatment and what the client should be doing for his or her part of the process, the more likely the client is to derive benefit from the process. He says the worker has three tasks when preparing to work on an involuntary basis: *(1)* identify non negotiable requirement from legally involuntary clients, *(2)* identify negotiable options and free choices, *(3)* monitor his/her feelings about the alleged offence. Supervisors also need to be involved in this preparation.

There may be some cases in which families may be more able to change if the statutory authority is not held by the professional who is directly attempting to induce the change. It may be particularly important for this professional not to be responsible for the planning, decision making, or direct work with the children. The worker can stress his/her comparative powerlessness in the decision making about the children and may then better be able to help parents take some responsibility for choices about what outcomes they would like and how this can be achieved. Kagan and Schlosberg (*1989*) suggest that this is helpful for families who are in perpetual crisis, have very low esteem and not trust in professional helpers. It is essential, however, that everyone working in this situation shares the same values and llong term goals and makes this clear to the family. Without this, the family conflicts are likely to be replayed in the professional group (*Dale et al*).

It will probably be necessary for multi disciplinary groups to undertake some work to try and achieve agreement in advance about how to proceed in both voluntary and involuntary situations and to consider what framework is necessary for this and who will do what. Kagan and Schlosberg suggest for example that a strong child protective service presence can create anxiety in a family that leads to change. The family worker can then nurture and support the needy parent(s) in making the change. Conferences are critical times for coordinating work and recognising the role of each practitioner with the family.

Social workers and other professionals will need help in these situations to prevent them from becoming incorporated into the family's emotional process. It is therefore critical for family workers to be able to step back and view their work with a consultant and/or a supervisor. This is particularly important as there are now many social workers who have little experience of providing treatment, and what perhaps is even more important, there are many managers who lack the experience and skill to supervise their staff in this area. The consultant/supervisor will also need to attend planning and decision making meetings to assist both the process for the worker and the objectivity of the decision making.

Using the legal process

The Children Act will require local authorities to be clear about their reasons and purposes for invoking the legal process. Furniss (*1991*) suggests that child abuse needs to be seen as both a children's rights issue and as a health and mental health problem. Child protective agencies and legal professionals intervene from a rights perspective to protect children from abuse and to punish perpetrators for the crime, whereas mental health workers want to set up treatment programmes to deal with the psychological sequelae of the abuse. He says the reasons for intervening may therefore be legal or therapeutic or a mixture of both but it is essential to distinguish between the two aspects and clarify the relationship between them. Some professionals, in his view, are unable to use the therapeutic potential of the crisis they create when they intervene on a legal level and this may result in 'abuse promoting child protection.' Other mental health professionals often do not know how to deal with the legal tasks of child protection and further crime prevention.

The emphasis on working on a voluntary basis wherever possible, under the new Act, would seem to be mainly for therapeutic reasons. If, however, the normative and crime prevention aspects are ignored, it may be much harder to establish appropriate standards of parental care and behaviour in future and to help parents to accept that what they may have done is wrong and needs to be changed. This may make it harder for local authorities to fulfil their statutory duty to reduce the amount of child abuse in their area. It may therefore be very important that decisions about taking a case to court are not based solely on therapeutic considerations about the child. Care proceedings could be taken to establish the threshold criteria even if no order is sought. Alternatively criminal proceedings could be taken against the perpetrator, particularly where there is a high risk of further abuse against other children, as in sexual abuse.

Conclusion

In order to promote the welfare of children primarily within their own families, local authorities will no longer be able to protect children merely by removing them from exposure to harm. As the Guidance (*Vol 2*) states, "this will require local authorities to rethink fundamentally their provision of services". In future, protection for children will need to be provided mainly though preventive services and adequate help and treatment for families already in difficulties.

The research makes it clear that to be effective services need to be matched appropriately with the particular child and family. Careful consideration needs to be given to 'who does what, with, or for, whom' Solutions to problems will not necessarily occur only thorough remedying deficits in the environment. The interaction between personality, relationships and the environment needs to be recognised. This will require the development of good assessment services and a range of treatment facilities for some families with complex problems as well as the development of community supports and services. All the services will need to reflect the needs of different racial, cultural and religious groups within the area. In order to provide these services staff will need knowledge and skills. They will also need training, support and time to do the work. Unless local authorities recognise the need to develop these services and the quality and human resources required to sustain them, it may not be possible to fulfil the aims of the Children Act and to protect children adequately.

Bibliography

Dale, P., Davies, M., Morrison, T., Waters, J. (1986) *Dangerous Families*. Tavistock.

Farmer, E., Parker, R. (1991). *Trials and Tribulations. A Study of Children Home on Trial in Four Local Authorities*. HMSO.

Furniss, T. (1991). *The Multi Professional Handbook of Child Sexual Abuse. Integrated Management, Therapy and Legal Intervention*. Routledge.

Jones, D.P.H. (1991). Professional and clinical challenges to the protection of children. *Child Abuse & Neglect* **Vol 15 Suppl 1**.

Kagan, R., Schlosberg, S. (1989). *Families in Perpetual Crisis*. Norton.

Martin, H. (1976). *The Abused Child. A Multi Disciplinary Approach to Developmental Issues and Treatment*. Ballinger.

Morrison, T. (1990). *The Professional Dilemma*. Child & Family Participation at Case Conferences, unpublished paper given at Newcastle University.

Rooney, R. (1988). Socialisation strategies for involuntary clients. Social case work. *The Journal of Contemporary Social Work*. Family Service America.

Rowe, J. (1991). *Patterns and Outcomes in Child Placement. Messages from current research and their implications.*. HMSO.

Rushton, A., Treseder, J., Quinton, D. (1988). *New Parents for Older Children*. BAAF.

Sainsbury, E. (1975). *Social Work with Families*. Routledge, Keegan and Paul.

Ward, H., Jackson, S. (1991). Developing outcome measures in child care. *British Journal of Social Work*. **Vol 21 No 4**.

Wells, K., Biegel, D. (1991). *Family Preservation Services. Research and Intervention.* Sage.

Significant harm in context

Dr Arnon Bentovim, Consultant Psychiatrist, Hospital for Sick Children,
Great Ormond Street, The Tavistock Clinic

Introduction

The notion of significant harm is an essential one in the making of a care
or supervision order. It is important to look at what it comprises, and to
consider other aspects of the issues involved. Harm itself is now defined
not only in terms of traditional notions of ill treatment – that is physical
abuse – but also includes sexual abuse which may show no physical
effects, and non physical ill treatment such as emotional abuse. It also
includes the impairment of health or development where health implies
physical or mental health, and development is not only physical, but also
includes intellectual, emotional, social or behavioural development.

It may be useful to think of significant harm generally as a compilation of
significant events, both acute and long-standing, which interact with the
child's ongoing development, and interrupt, alter, or impair physical and
psychological development. Being the victim of significant harm is likely
to have a profound effect on a child's view of themselves as a person, and on
their future lives. Significant harm represents a major symptom of failure
of adaptation by parents to their role, and also involves both the family
and society.

Categories of harm

It is usual to think in terms of:

Physical abuse – Physical injury to a child where there is a definite knowledge, or a reasonable suspicion, that the injury was inflicted or not
knowingly prevented. This also includes the induction of illness states
through the administration of medications, or noxious substances.

Neglect – The persistent or severe neglect of a child which results in
serious impairment of that child's health or development. This may take
the form of exposure to danger, or repeated failure to attend to the

physical and/or developmental needs of a child. An alternative form is failure to thrive without organic cause, resulting from the neglect of a child.

Emotional abuse – The persistent emotional ill treatment of a child which has a severe adverse effect on the behaviour and emotional development of that child.

Sexual abuse – The involvement of dependent, immature children and adolescents in sexual activities that they do not really comprehend, to which they are unable to give informed consent, which violate the social taboos of family life, and are knowingly not prevented by the carer.

Definitions for the purpose of registration can be found in Working Together (1991) but it is noted in Working Together that the definitions offered there "do not tie in precisely with the definition of 'significant harm' in Section 31 of the Children Act".

Levels of abuse

It is helpful to think of each category in terms of the severity of the abuse. (*See figure 1 opposite.*)

There is clearly a difference in approaching the least severe forms of abuse. There would be an expectation of agencies working together in such cases with the use of child protection registration, working on a voluntary basis in partnership with parents and a variety of different agencies to offer appropriate assistance. However even lesser forms of abuse, such as exhibitionism or sexual fondling, can have major implications because the abuse may be associated with a basic paedophiliac orientation, and may require protective action of a different magnitude to a child who has a mild degree of neglect, or is living in a critical scapegoating atmosphere.

Where moderate levels of abuse are present the implication for the longer-term mental and physical health of the child without appropriate intervention is far more doubtful. There may well need to be a higher level of protective action, such as the use of interim care orders or interim supervision orders during a period of longer-term assessment of the

Least severe	Moderate abuse	Severe abuse
Bruising, no fractures in an older child	Bruising in a baby, fractures not including head and neck	Fractures, multiple, over a period of time, different sites, particularly with fractures around the head and neck in a baby under 6 months
Weight parallel rather than markedly below third centile	Growth failure, but not lengthy, basically of weight	Severe non-organic failure to thrive with stunting in both length and weight
Mild degrees of neglect without major failure to care, and family chaos	Failure of care, moderate degrees of deprivation and neglect	Severe neglect, deprivation state, skin, hair changes, severe accidents due to poor supervision
Critical, scapegoating, confusing atmosphere, emotional disorder without major conduct problems	Rejection, privation but with tendencies towards conduct problems rather than frozen regression and retardation	Severe rejection resulting in pseudo-autistic, regresses states of frozen watchfulness, pseudo-retardation
Sexual exhibitionism	Sexual abuse, shorter duration, fondling and/or oral contact	Sexual abuse, long-standing, involving attempted or actual genital or anal intercourse, particularly in younger children associated with gross physical signs, major sexualised patterns
	Fabrication of symptoms leading to investigation	Induction of illness of such severity that life is threatened – eg suffocation, attempted drowning.

figure 1

parent's capacity to provide more appropriate care. When abuse has this level of severity, Section 8 orders covering a variety of contact, residence, prohibited steps or specific issues may be necessary, in addition to the supervision order.

Severe abuse is also going to require higher levels of protection during the assessment process. There are likely to be cases where care orders or residence orders and carefully managed contact will be necessary.

Psychosocial difficulties associated with significant harm

Patterns of abusive behaviour or harmful attitudes may develop in parents as a result of the interaction of the intellectual and emotional characteristics and behaviour of the parent(s) and the demands of the child and the outside world at a particular time. In understanding a particular case, family attributes and parental care must be assessed both in terms of their connection with the pattern of abuse, but also in terms of the possibility of change: the potential for providing adequate competent care in the future. It is usual to consider the physical and psychiatric health of the parents, and to define any adult psychiatric syndromes present. The intellectual potential of the parents, their functioning, and parenting ability must also be considered. Assessment must be made of their ability to provide an adequate affective atmosphere, warmth, nurturance and a caring relationship. The patterns of alliances that are created within the family, and the expectations of family members, must be considered along with the boundaries of the family, that is, the parents' capacity to maintain the line between themselves and the child, and their ability to communicate and share with the children. Further aspects of the assessment should include parents' competence in carrying out tasks, their ability to relate to professionals in the outside world, and their relationships with neighbourhood and extended family.

Recognised stress factors which may contribute to physical harm or psychiatric disturbance in the child and therefore to significant emotional harm, include:

parental psychiatric disturbance;

discordant intrafamilial relations;

lack of warmth in intrafamilial relations;

familial over involvement;

inadequate or inconsistent parental control;

inadequate living conditions;

inadequate or distorted intrafamilial communications;

anomalous family situations.

All of these and a variety of other major stressful factors can affect parental behaviour, and result in over-punitive attitudes, rejection, escalation of aversive, negative interactions, and perception of the child as deserving rejection or abuse.

Family health scales have been developed to describe family functions (*Kinston et al, 1987*). There are a number of areas which specifically focus on parenting. Figure 2 illustrates these. There are 4 levels of functioning. Optimal and adequate functioning describe family contexts which should be good enough to ensure appropriate nurturance and adequate socialisation. Dysfunctional and breakdown levels describe contexts which put children at serious risk of significant harm if they continue and the standard of care does not improve.

Understanding and establishing significant harm

To understand and establish the significant harm criteria in s31 it is necessary to consider:

1. The family context in which significant harm occurs.

2. The process of the development of the child in this context.

3. The nature of significant harm in terms of ill treatment and its effects on development with or without intervention.

4. The nature of significant impairment which includes developmental issues, physical factors, parental contributions, and other factors and comparison with a similar child.

5. The link with an assessment of parental care, and what it is reasonable to expect of parents.

figure 2	Breakdown	Dysfunctional
Pattern of relationships	Serious deficiencies; marked splits, scapegoating, severe triangulation, or isolation of all family members	Serious discord or distance between members, or shifting or exclusive alignments. Children repeatedly detour parental tension or conflicts.
Marital relationship	Destructive relationship, for example, couple fused, at war or isolated from one another	Overt marital difficulties; or both partners dissatisfied.
Parental relationship	Parents not working together at all, or extremely weak, divisive or conflicted relationship	Parents repeatedly disagree, act without reference to one another, or one parent repeatedly takes over or opts out
Parent–child relationship	Both parents reject, ignore, exploit, continuously attack or disqualify a child	Parental attitudes and behaviours are clearly unsupportive or harmful; poor understanding of the children
Child–parent relationship	Children avoid, reject, continually oppose, or cling to parent(s); or show marked differentiation in their attitudes to each parent	One or more children show oppositional, withdrawn, over-dependent or domineering behaviour towards parent(s)
Sibling relationships	Sibs fight continuously or ignore each other; extreme rivalry and competition for the parents' attention	Obvious discord or distance between the sibs.

Adequate	Optimal
Satisfactory relationships but with greater closeness or distance between some family members than others	The nature and strength of relationships between family members is constructive and appropriate to their respective ages and roles
Basically satisfactory with some areas of discontent	Mature relationship; warm, supportive, affectionate, emphatic, compatible; couple work together well
Basic agreement on child-rearing but with some deficiencies in support and/or working together	Strong parental coalition; agreement and cooperation in child-rearing; sharing of pleasure and mutual support
Parents support children and enjoy being with them but with minor or occasional problems in relating to the children	Parents show care and concern; understand and pay attention to children appropriately; and are ready to participate in their activities
Child–parent relationships are secure, but with mild difficulties in some areas or between particular dyads.	Children relate to both parents; are cooperative yet spontaneous; feel safe and show appropriate dependence.
Sibs affiliate with some limited rivalry, quarrelling or lack of contact.	Sibs interact freely with shared enjoyment, affection, concern; differences can be resolved.

Descriptions from the 'Alliances mainscale' of the family health scales, which considers the relationships and coalitions amongst family members (Kinston et al 1987).

The family context and significant harm

The family is an organisation, which has grown up to meet the needs of the individuals within it. Competent partnering implies the meeting of adult needs for support, affection and sexuality and competent parenting implies the provision of adequate nurturance, care, warmth, stimulation and socialisation of children.

A 'Good Enough' parent provides:

- adequate verbal communication to give information and intellectual stimulation;

- sufficient physical freedom to encourage the development of the child's sensory and motor abilities;

- adequate responsiveness which balances the child's need for attention to his or her behaviour, and the needs of the parent;

- positive warmth and a loving framework.

This tempers the child's demands and helps the child learn to be self regulatory rather than requiring external monitoring (*Maccoby and Martin, 1983*).

It is important to consider the nature of the family and to see it as an organisation which has strengths to nurture, care and socialise, but also to be aware of inherent problems within the organisation which make it liable to develop interactions which can be sufficiently harmful to require professional intervention.

Families are prone to stress. Families are constantly undergoing changes or transitions. The life cycle, birth of children, maturation, aging, retirement, death, represent major events which can have effects on the family and on the parents' capacity to care. Similarly, events affecting individuals eg unemployment, illness, handicap, may cause stress to be transmitted to other family members. Violent means of dealing with stress is a characteristic learned response and may be transmitted within the family. The question is not whether the family is an institution prone to violence and conflict, but how much there is and whether the effects create a family context which is significantly harmful to the children within it. Gelles and

Strauss (1979) have pinpointed a number of such factors in their research.

Privacy

The modern family is a private institution, insulated from the eyes, the ears and often enough the rules of wider society. Social control by definition must therefore be low. Idiosyncratic rules and family meanings grow in isolation. Appropriate ways of expressing both violence and affection within the community can be distorted by personal interpretation and enacted in the family with little external influence. Although there is public outcry about mistreatment of children, there is still a reluctance to interfere in family life.

Development of the child

The unfolding of the various aspects of development is complex. Constitutional, genetic and environmental factors eg the effects of physical illness, injury and handicapping conditions and the family context in which the child grows up all play a part. Culture, class factors, and intergenerational effects which derive from the parents' own experiences of parenting may also be influential.

The importance of the child's development and the effect of significant harm on this has been described by Jones, Bentovim, Cameron, Vizard and Wolkind (*1990*) in their paper for the Judicial Studies Board training programme, revised at p.115 in this book.

"The developmental perspective emphasises the unfolding of the individual over time, in physical, social and psychological spheres of life. The process consists of a series of basic tasks which, once achieved by the child, remain critical for the individual throughout life. Each critical task may not be so obvious as life unfolds and new tasks become relatively more prominent. Each sphere of development inter-relates and influences the others. Developmental medicine is concerned with understanding these processes in sickness or in health. This approach also emphasises that a single individual may change dramatically over time in either direction and the developmental approach is to identify key mechanisms with which to understand the individual's development, as well as to identify potential influences which might encourage the individual towards health and away from the direction of sickness.

Key tasks of social and emotional development are:

i   the baby's achievement of a balanced state, eg feeding, sleeping and elimination (*During first few weeks of life*)

ii   the development of a secure attachment with a caretaker (*During 0–12 months of age*)

iii the development of an independent sense of self (*During 12–30 months*)

iv   the establishment of peer relationships (*30 months–7 years*)

v   the integration of attachment, independence and peer relationships (*7–12 years*)

(*age in brackets denotes when the task is most prominent but the achievement continues to be important to the individual*)

Not all abused children go on to become damaged children or damaged adults. We tend to see those who do repeat the cycle, but a study of those who do not repeat the cycle has taught us a great deal, For example, the importance of good 'corrective' relationships, success in school, skill, craft, art, physical performance, and the positive benefit of therapy and understanding of the meaning of maltreatment have all been identified as factors which mark out those whose future adjustment is better despite early deprivation and abuse. Thus few single influences on development, including severe abuse, have an inevitable future consequence, and all factors have the potential to affect future outcome in the direction of good or less good states of adjustment. Additionally, the sum as well as direction of such influences may alter over the individual's life course, so that a disturbed child can change, if there is sufficient change in the positive and negative influences bearing on him/her."

Attachment

Jones et al have also described attachment.

"**Definitions and characteristics:** Attachment is a particular form of relationship. Its major characteristics are that it provides a base from which a child can explore the world and that the presence of a person to whom the child is attached reduces the child's anxiety in stressful situations. Attachment lays the foundations for the ability to make lasting relationships and to cope confidently with new situations (*Bowlby, 1969*).

Assessment of attachment: It is assessed by seeing how the presence of attachment figures allows the child to cope with unfamiliar surroundings and with the presence of strangers. The way the child reacts to the departure and return of the parent is an important part of the procedure (*Ainsworth et al, 1978*).

The course of attachment: During the first six months babies begin to distinguish important figures in their life, but any adult, familiar or strange, can usually soothe distress. They can be moved from one caretaker to another with relatively little difficulty. From six to eighteen months infants become increasingly selective. They become upset at attention from strangers and are distressed when their attachment figures leave them. Though the fear of strangers diminishes, the obvious need for the attachment to adults remains very obvious until around age three. After this age the child, with greater intellectual development, can more easily understand why an attachment figure has to leave and will be less distressed by separations.

Breaks in attachment: The loss of the primary figure between the ages of six months to three years can be followed by profound distress. The child can establish new attachments, but often only with great difficulty and much testing behaviour. Multiple breaks can lead to the child being virtually unable to make true relationships. Such children are noticeable by their indiscriminate over friendliness to adults (*Bowlby, 1973 & 1980*).

The quality of attachment: Severely abused children can show strong clinging to their parents. Strength of clinging is not a good measure of attachment. The key is the ability of the attachment relationship to provide the two components of increasing confidence and reducing anxiety. Different qualities of attachment can be seen: secure or insecure. With an insecure attachment, the child hardly notices the departure and return of the parent, or alternatively even in his or her presence remains frozen and unable to explore a new environment. Insecure attachment is associated with later problems in relationships. The insecurely attached child may show little distress after a permanent removal though the development of new attachments may take a long time.

The antecedents of attachment: The term 'attachment' describes a type of relationship between two people. To develop securely it requires contributions from both parents and child. Most children without severe brain damage have the capacity to form attachments. Two factors impair an adult's ability to reciprocate: their own childhood experience and the quality of relationships they have with others. The parent who received very poor parenting and who has no close relationships with other adults may be very insensitive to the meaning of cues given by their babies and this can lead to an insecure attachment pattern. Parents with a psychiatric disorder which impairs their sensitivity may also have major difficulties. The situation is however never static. Changes in the parents' circumstances can lead to changes in the quality of attachment.

Legal issues and attachment: Knowledge of the course of attachment emphasises the crucial nature of the timescale in legal disputes eg removing a child before six months as opposed to waiting until they are one year older.

The knowledge may need to be applied when suggestions are made about removing a child from an adult with whom it has a secure attachment. This could be where a biological parent has difficulties in caring for the child, perhaps through illness. It could also be where 'a short term' foster parent has, because of delays, kept the child throughout the crucial period.

The presence of an insecure attachment may be an important factor when deciding whether parents can meet the needs of a particular child."

There is a strong association between child abuse during infancy and early childhood and an insecure attachment with the care giver (*Ainsworth, 1980; Egeland & Sroufe, 1981; Crittenden, 1988*).

Disorganised attachments

There can also be a major disruption of attachment if, for example, the parents are unable to maintain consistency, predictability and a physical presence. Frequently placement of a child with alternative caretakers or situations where partners split up, or leave precipitously can induce extreme insecurity and a lack of sense of safety.

Disorganisation may also occur if a parent has severe psychiatric or physical illness and there are frequent absences during significant periods of the child's development. The period of maximum sensitivity for attachment which needs to be met is generally accepted as between four months and to the end of the third year of life. This is the period when the child has least capacity to understand what is happening, has most need of secure attachment figures and is most prone to develop insecure attachments which can have longlasting effects (*Bowlby, 1976 & 1980*). For example, when mothers are depressed over this sensitive period children show failures to explore some 18 months later (*Murray, 1991*).

Securely attached children show considerable disturbance if separation has to occur from primary figures. There is however a potential to form a new deeper attachment following mourning. By contrast an insecurely attached child will often show little response to separation from a rejecting or abusing parent. They will attach to a new parenting figure with apparent ease. However, longstanding patterns of expecting and provoking punishment, sexualisation, aggressive and regressive patterns will soon emerge after the honeymoon.

Although placements of older children can be made and good attachments formed (*Tizard & Hodges, 1978, and Hodges & Tizard, 1989*), there is a greater possibility of breakdown the longer the period of disrupted attachments and the larger the number of different caretakers that the child has had. Considering the child's sense of time and needs means making decisions within the child's time frame rather than the adult's and ensuring stability and security of attachment at the earliest opportunity (*Goldstein, Freud and Solnit, 1979 & 1979; Goldstein, Freud, Solnit and Goldstein, 1986*).

Parenting roles and identifications

Associated with major disruption of attachments is the induction of children into particular roles within the family, and the need for the child to respond to particular relationship demands. Individuals who themselves have had major deficits in their own parenting characteristically see in the birth of a new baby a hope both of a child to love, and to make up for past failures. There may be an expectation that the child will supply the emotional needs not met through earlier life experiences or through relationship with a partner. Alternatively women with an absence of good memories of their own childhood may focus their lives on caretaking and put the care of others and the care of their own children ahead of their need as partners in their adult relationships (*Monck et al, 1991*).

The danger is that children, because of their own needs can make demands that overwhelm the resources of such parents. This means that frustration, resentment and grievance are almost inevitable. There is a risk of rejection, abuse and a recreation of the very pattern of abuse the parent had been avoiding.

The significance of harm

Significant harm may be defined as the state of a child which is attributable to ill treatment or failure to provide adequate care. To understand and demonstrate the significance of the harm, we have to consider in detail the effect of ill treatment and inadequate care on the child's development. There is no specific pattern of response to particular forms of maltreatment, but there are non specific signs and symptoms of developmental deviation resulting from the child's trauma.

Significant harm can be seen as the effect of ill treatment and poor care on the potential of the child to develop along the lines described earlier in comparison with the development of a similar child.

Significant harm may also represent a traumatic event in the child's life.

Trauma is a Greek word meaning 'to pierce'. It is most often used in the context of physical injury, where the skin is broken – where something once intact has been breached. It suggests that the event which creates the breach is of a certain intensity or violence – and consequences to the organism are long standing. From the physical notion of trauma arises the notion of trauma as an event which in the same intense or violent way ruptures the protective layer that surrounds the mind, with equally long-lasting consequences for psychic organisation (*Garland, 1991*).

A sense of helplessness overwhelms the individual; mastery, control and defence fails, and there is a sense of being unprotected, of disintegration and acute mental pain. Although significant harm can take the form of acute single overwhelming events, they are often repeated, frequent and in a context of rejection, anger and failure to respond to the core of the child's being.

Traumatic events are a specific form of severe stress – where stress is defined as a "disequilibrating event which temporarily disturbs the functioning of the individual and initiates a chain of adaptive or maladaptive responses" (*Wolfe, 1987*). Pynoos and Eth (*1985*) have described the Post Traumatic Stress Disorder in children, which is defined as responses to particular events.

1. The traumatic event is persistently re-experienced in at least one of: recurrent intrusive and distressing recollection or dreams, re-experiencing action or feelings (traumatic play), extensive distress at reminders.

2. There may be a persistent avoidance of stimuli associated with trauma or numbing of general responsiveness.

3. There may be persistent symptoms of increased arousal, irritability, sleep difficulties, excessive vigilance, startled response, reactions to reminders of stress.

4. Usually the onset is immediately following the traumatic event.

Trauma can be longstanding and associated with extreme stress. It is associated with very strong denial and dissociation; extensive numbing; self-doubt, insecurity, elevated fears, anxiety and a sense of rage which bursts through at times; and an unremitting sense of sadness as personality style (*Terr, 1991*).

The infant and growing child has to adapt and cope with these experiences to survive psychologically. Personal constructions or attributions have to be formed in a search for meanings for uncontrollable events. Children may either blame themselves or some feature or person in the outside world. Abnormal attachment patterns, ambivalent clinging and fighting, aversive turning away from the parent, the dazed, anxious or disorientated attitude of the disrupted child, all represent ways of coping. Such distorted patterns of relating come to be represented in the child's mind as a 'model of the world' and to organise his way of responding (*Crittenden, 1988*).

Psychologically children may have to develop a shell implying total self-sufficiency, so that throughout the stages of development when the child should be becoming peer worthy and relating to other adults, he presents himself as being without needs and may be seen as aloof, distant and without empathy. This has devastating effects on the long term ability to relate both as a child, young person and later as a parent (*Bentovim & Kinston, 1991*).

Another response may be the compliant, victim role associated with a process of identification with the aggressor. The child may appear to seek punishment, and as time goes on, become involved in relationships which perpetuate abuse.

A distressing response may be that of identification with the abuser. The child becomes manipulative, controlling, hostile and combative instead of responsive and receptive.

Figure 3 shows the way in which such traumatic experiences can affect the childhood and adolescence of individuals and their ability to be parents to their own children in subsequent generations. Parenting, to be

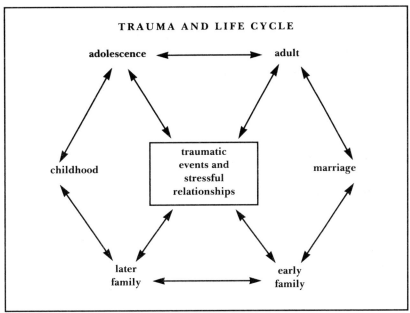

TRAUMA AND LIFE CYCLE

figure 3

competent, requires the development of empathy; the ability to be able to read the emotional cues of the other; to put ones own needs aside and focus on the needs of children; to be appropriately firm and ensure that social rules are learnt and maintained. The long term experience of abuse during childhood and adolescence may affect the development of these parental skills in a devastating way. It can result in an authoritarian style of parenting, insensitivity to the child's level of ability, or needs, combined with the excessive demands, use of power and assertive techniques which are characteristic of physically abusive parents (*La Rose & Wolfe, 1987*).

Protective factors

There are protective factors which can mitigate against such responses and there is a significant degree of plasticity or resilience in development (*Rutter, 1983*). This depends in part on the response of significant adults and their ability to exert control and efficacy in the midst of confusion and upheaval. It depends too on the earlier history, for example, of attachments, which may have provided a rehearsal and practice for later defences against stressful events (*Lipsell, 1983*). Intervention, treatment, placement in positive environments, even the making of more satisfactory relationships in adulthood can neutralise some of the potentially harmful long term effects. Not all physically, or sexually, abused children become abusive adults although there is a higher risk (3–5 times as high) in comparison with adults who were not abused.

Significant harm and physical abuse

Significant physical harm occurs either as a result of neglect or failure to care, implying a failure of protection on the parents' part, or the commission of physical harm through inappropriate punitiveness, or desire to hurt and inflict pain. Physical abuse usually occurs in a context of an abusive atmosphere within the home. High levels of punitiveness, unexpected pain and hurt, the misuse of power and authority involved in physical abuse also have major effects on the behavioural pattern of the child (*Maccoby & Martin, 1983*). Figure 4 shows the effects of frequent misuse of power (*Spinetta & Rigler, 1972*).

There is a connection between the sense of powerlessness, resulting from invasion of the body, vulnerability, absence of protection and a repeated fear and helplessness. This can result in fear, anxiety and an inability to control events, along with learning difficulties, despair, depression and low sense of efficacy seen as 'frozen watchfulness'. This sense of helplessness may lead to the development of a need to control and dominate, or to aggressive, abusive patterns, or the development of 'a shell' to ward off feelings about the other person (*George & Main, 1979*).

Behaviours indicative of poor self control have been described by Gaensbauer & Sands (*1979*). They include distractability, negative emotions, low enthusiasm, resistance to direction.

Within the school, patterns of behaviour may include attention seeking, extremely provocative behaviour to adults and bullying. Ultimately there may be a major rejection of the child. Such behavioral patterns are grouped together as the psychiatric disorder of 'conduct problems'. The children are perceived as difficult to manage, less socially mature, re-

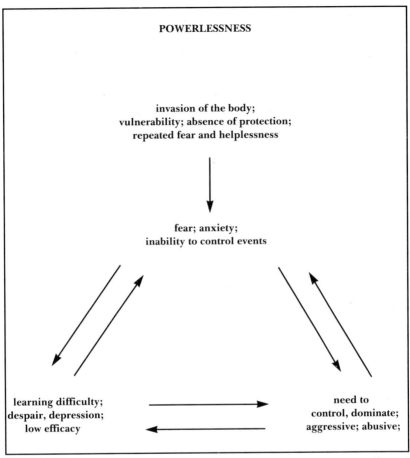

POWERLESSNESS

invasion of the body;
vulnerability; absence of protection;
repeated fear and helplessness

fear; anxiety;
inability to control events

learning difficulty;
despair, depression;
low efficacy

need to
control, dominate;
aggressive; abusive;

figure 4

jected by peers, deficient in social skills, and liable to commit violent criminal acts (*Herrenkohl et al, 1984*).

If moderate or severe abuse continues over a long period, responses may be seen such as depressive states, hopelessness, self injurious behaviour, pica, enuresis and encopresis.

When describing physical abuse it is essential to bear in mind the effect of the 'abusive context'. The atmosphere of punitiveness, rejection, criticism, scapegoating, belittling, may in turn induce the frozen compliant response, or the provocative angry response which justifies the parents' continuing criticism and anger. There may be perpetuation of the cycle through bullying of other children. Furthermore, there is evidence from epidemiological surveys to show the effect of punitiveness in one generation being repeated in terms of propensity to use bullying or physically punitive responses in the next generation. These children may be seen as 'out of control' or rejecting parental care (*Gelles & Strauss, 1979*).

Significant harm and emotional abuse

Garbarino et al (*1978*) define emotional or psychological abuse as the destruction of the child's competence to be able to function in social situations. Being denied appropriate contact with peers within or outside school, and being forced to take on a particular role in relation to parents, can therefore be seen as having a major destructive effect on the child's competence to function in social contexts. When parents have a psychiatric illness a major concern is the adult's involvement of the child in their psychotic process, such as, a shared delusionary state or paranoid beliefs (*Rutter, 1966*).

Parents can feel as if they are the abused children rather than vice versa. Children can be inducted into parental caretaking roles, and may not be encouraged to be involved in appropriate play, relationships with peers, and development of a true self. The extreme of the parental role occurs when there is incestuous abuse and the use of the child as a sexual partner whether by father or mother, inducting the male or female child into a parental or partner role inappropriately (*Bentovim et al, 1988*).

In marital breakdown one parent may use a child as partner against the other parent, and the attachment relationship is disrupted with the other parent. There is a potential for the creation of a rejecting, resentful, relationship with that other parent with blaming and fault finding destroying what may have been a good enough relationship. Accusations of abuse by the other parent can further undermine the potential for developing a secure attachment with both parents, despite separations. It is important to consider whether such situations result in the child suffering significant harm.

Adaptation to parental lifestyles may also cause significant harm, eg where children become part of a parents' drug culture, prostitution or other antisocial activities, and become confused in terms of socialisation into the appropriate moral views of what are appropriate societal values. The boundary between a lifestyle and airing the family beliefs versus being persuaded to use drugs, become prostituted, or involved in direct antisocial acts, may be a fine one and depends on a comprehensive assessment of the child and family.

Significant harm and illness induction

Munchausen Syndrome, where adults either medicate themselves or de-scribe symptoms which then result in medical investigation or surgical intervention, can also be seen in the child. In recent years there has been major concern about children who are actually induced into illness states by the administration of medications (*non-accidental poisoning, Rogers et al, 1976*) or are perceived and described as having symptoms which require investigation, particularly fits and faints: Munchausen Syndrome by Proxy (*Meadow, 1982*).

Bools and Meadow (*1991*) confirmed earlier work by Rogers et al (*1976*) in seeing the parents as needing an ill child for their own marital or personal mental health needs. There may be a deeply ambivalent view of the child, a failure to attach at the time of pregnancy because the child was unwanted, or the parent themselves had experienced earlier rejec-tion and failed to attach in a secure way to the infant. The parent may feel the child is literally taking over her life: the child is gradually experienced as a persecutory figure who deserves to be hurt, or used as an ill child to gain sympathy and support given to such a parent. Again this is use of the child as a thing and not as a person.

A child subject to repeated unnecessary medical investigations may suffer unnecessary pain and risk, and if inappropriate treatments are given they can have dangerous side effects – a manifestation of significant harm. For a child to see themselves as having a major handicapping condition or disability or take on an invalid role when there is a normal potential for health is also a cause of significant harm.

It is essential to understand the processes which lead to this unusual abusive action, so that there can be an assessment of the capacity of the parent to acknowledge the degree of potential harm, and to use appropriate help to be able to nurture and protect the child and to be able to reverse harmful effects.

Significant harm, growth and development

A diagnosis of failure to thrive can only be made if it can be shown that there has been a failure to give sufficient nutrition. Skuse (*1991*) has drawn attention to the fact that considerable care must be exercised in making the diagnosis as there are many other factors which can result in failure to grow as well as failure to provide adequate nutrition. Skuse (*1991*) has also indicated that what is now called retardation of linear growth in older children, formerly known as psychosocial dwarfism, needs to be differentiated from failure to thrive. Psychosocial dwarfism is associated with lack of secure attachment in the form of warm physical contact which has detrimental effects on growth regulation.

Failure to thrive babies respond well to the provision of nutrition by tube feeding or by different handling of feeding. The test is whether the parent can ensure that the child can continue growing and thriving. Major retardation of linear growth – psychosocial dwarfism – also shows a striking reversal in another context. In hospital or foster home there can often be a quite striking growth, with considerable acceleration and catching up. There is now evidence (*Skuse, 1991*) that prolonged growth failure during the early years has a detrimental affect on brain development. This is shown by failure in the development of cognitive abilities and achieving the potential intellectual level. This represents significant harm to the child.

Severe neglect, deprivation, failure to provide adequate care, nutrition, stimulation can be associated with a sense of parental hopelessness and helplessness as described by Polansky et al (*1981*).

Severe neglect is associated with major retardation of cognitive functioning as well as growth. It is recognised through a typical pattern of poor hair growth, (skin effects), growth failure, poor hygiene, withdrawal and in extreme situations a pseudo-autistic state, all of which can rapidly reverse in alternative care.

Major growth failure, cognitive impairment, eg poor attention and concentration and associated learning difficulties can become a structural feature of the child's cognitive and developmental functioning. There may well be failure within school and there is a well tested association between conduct problems and learning difficulties within school eg reading, and educational failure.

There is often a striking reversal of neglect patterns when the child is in a different context and the question again is whether the parent can be helped through his or her sense of hopelessness or helplessness towards a new ability to provide adequate stimulation to ensure growth and development rather than failure and deprivation.

Although neglect has one of the most pervasive effects on development and is one of the most frequent forms of abuse, it is an area which is neglected by professionals – the neglect of neglect. Professionals, like the parents, may feel hopeless and overwhelmed by large families living in very poor conditions, with very little social support.

Sexual abuse

The traumatic effects of child sexual abuse can be summarised by stating that there are multiple affective, cognitive and behavioral effects and such effects persist. The earlier the disruptions occur, the more adversely subsequent phases of development may be affected. The child develops coping mechanisms which were described earlier, for example, shell development to avoid thinking, a compliant victim role, or angry aggressive responses which become stable and result in personality disorders, which shape later relationships and future mental health.

The immediate post-traumatic stress disorder associated with sexual abuse was described by McCleer (*1988*) from a series of young children who had been abused within a day nursery. The descriptions are as follows:

- re-experiencing, where children were observed to talk about abuse, playing out abusive patterns;

- flashbacks and nightmares;

- indulging in inappropriate sexual activity;

- memories occurring in places or with people and objects associated with the abuse and considered to be symbolic of them;

- visualisation, drawing, day dreaming their experiences;

- avoidant responses associated with the avoidance of people, places and things associated with abuse.

Children were often fearful of going into particular houses or rooms, or were fearful of people who reminded the child of the abuser, perhaps of a particular gender, eg dislike of men or older people. Associated with this was an often extreme unwillingness to talk about abuse, and evidence of a deletion – a hole in the mind – and a total lack of memory, even wiping out of memories earlier than the abuse itself.

The children also had difficulties falling or staying asleep, often associated with anxieties about going to sleep, irritable aggressive behaviour which was a reversal of the previous passive sense of having to be involved with abuse, distractibility and difficulty in concentrating and a degree of hyperalertness shown by anxiety or being easily startled. (These symptoms are described as autonomic hyperarousal.)

Longer term effects of sexual abuse

The longer abuse continues, the more extensive it is, for example involving penetrative abuse, the older the child, and the greater the number of stages that abuse continues through, the more disturbed the child is likely to be, the more depressed and sad, and the greater their loss of self esteem. Self esteem is the way in which an individual thinks of himself, for example how good or how bad he is. Children who have suffered chronic long-term sexual abuse feel very negatively about themselves and all aspects of their relationships, and they have very high levels of distress. (*Monck et al, 1991; Friedrich, 1990; Terr, 1991*)

Longer term effects can be described in terms of what Finkelhor (*1987*) has called traumagenic dynamics. Figure 5, traumatic sexualisation en-

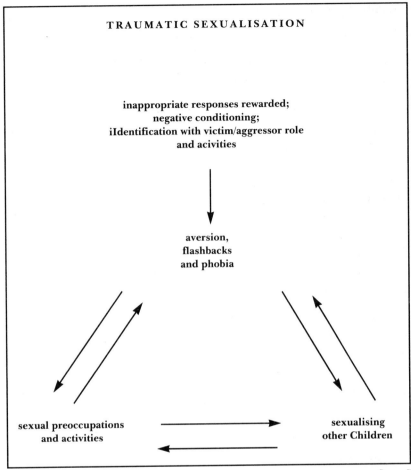

TRAUMATIC SEXUALISATION

inappropriate responses rewarded;
negative conditioning;
iIdentification with victim/aggressor role
and acivities

aversion,
flashbacks
and phobia

sexual preoccupations
and activities

sexualising
other Children

figure 5

larges the traumatic effects described earlier and leads to a cycle of avoidance of anything to do with sexuality, bursts of flashbacks and re-experiencing which continue for many years, sexual preoccupations, and sexually inappropriate behaviour with other children and adults. There is a significant difference in the responses of girls and boys. Girls tend to take a more compliant response, boys are more likely to externalise, to be aggressive and hostile and more likely to reenact abuse. Forty percent of those who abuse children sexually have themselves been abused in childhood. Others have suffered other forms of abuse – rejection, emotional abuse, physical abuse. Being treated as an object or a 'thing' means that the child treats others in a similar way and this pattern may persist in childhood and later development (*Bentovim, 1991*).

Poor self-esteem, self injurious behaviour and sexual abuse

One of the most worrying responses in older girls particularly those who have been abused are major depressive symptoms, poor self esteem and self worth and self injurious behaviour. There may be overdosing, wrist slashing, anorectic responses, re-enactment of abusive experiences, and gaining relief through hurt, suicidal attempts of self starvation, (*Bentovim et al, 1988*) and even 'total refusal syndromes' – withdrawal, refusal to eat, talk, or walk (*Lask et al, 1991*).

Another element which comes into the process of sexual abuse is the sense of betrayal and stigmatisation which children feel as a result of the threats, secrecy and self-justifying attitude of the abuser. Guilt and a low opinion of oneself, which may lead to drug and alcohol abuse, promiscuous seeking of redeeming relationships, and clinging to unstable partners can all be responses to the victimisation process.

There may be major dissociation and repression of traumatic responses until later stages of development when there can be profound effects on later sexual adjustment with avoidance and frozen responses, major problems in parenting and child birth and child care, and a vulnerability to longer term depression and anxiety (*Mullen et al, 1988*).

Protective factors

Children will not all suffer the same long term effects. One of the more important factors which dictates the extent of significant harm is how much support the child receives from family members after a disclosure is made. A mother's belief in her child's statements concerning abuse reduces the ill effects on the child. Children feel less depressed and feel better about themselves when they know that they are believed and supported by the parent who should be most supportive. Paradoxically therefore in sexual abuse the effects of abuse and the depth of harm depends both on the extent of abuse and the ability of the parent to respond with support and belief once that abuse has been disclosed. (*Monck et al, 1991*)

Friedrich (*1990*) stresses the importance of a comprehensive assessment of both the child and the family, which looks at the pre- as well as the post abuse functioning. He draws on the work of Rutter (*1983*) to identify the resilience and coping abilities of some children which may help to minimise some of the effects of sexual abuse.

Social-cognitive effects in significant harm

Many of the areas of abuse and failure of care described here can have major effects on the social-cognitive development of the individual. This may come about through the child having a particular role attributed to him, for example, being 'the bad one'. Children may identify themselves as having been responsible for their own abuse, for example, by provoking punitive responses. The sexually abused child's sexual preoccupations, flashbacks, poor self esteem can be pervasive, so that traumatic acts organise their cognitive reality and there may be failures in academic settings, failures of motivation, willingness to follow directions, poor self control (*Lynch & Roberts, 1982*).

Being in contact with confusing moral standards within the family has major effects on moral and societal knowledge, and the rules that govern interpersonal conduct. With such an impact on interpersonal relationships, particularly peer relationships, there are difficulties in being able to form confiding relationships and to develop intimate contacts in later life. There may be continuing confusion about others intentions – just as the neglected child may perceive friendly approaches as hostile, the physically abused may feel neutral responses to be hostile, the sexually abused may feel ordinary affection to be sexual approaches.

Conclusion

Significant harm can have major long term effects on all aspects of the child's development and functioning, behavioral, social- emotional, social cognitive and cognitive, as well as on physical development, growth and well being. It is not only the stressful events of abuse which are harmful, but the family context in which they occur.

Parenting which is inadequate or abusive, causing significant harm, occurs in families which fail to achieve the usual balance between positive and negative interactions, discipline and emotional bonding. There is a process whereby the families of origin of such parents may provide a 'training ground' for interpersonal violence and reduced social competence, through exposure to stressful and traumatic life events. This means they are ill prepared for the stresses of parenting, and their adaptation means that the child is seen as cause of anger, frustrations and arousal. Abusive patterns – physical, emotional and sexual – are triggered and these become part of the inflexible maladaptive breakdown state of the family.

There are mitigating and relieving factors; not all abused children go on to become abusing adults, not all abusive parents continue their aversive interactions with their children. Recognition of families at risk – parents and children, in the earliest processes of developing abusive patterns is essential in order to break the cycle of abuse and prevent damaging processes taking root.

Bibliography

Ainsworth, N.D., Blehar, M.C., Waters, E., Wall, S. (1978). *Patterns of Attachment: Assessed in the Strange Situation and at Home*. Hillside, N.J.: Lawrence Erlbaum.

Ainsworth, N.M. (1980). Attachment and Child Abuse. In G. Gerbner, C.J. Ross and E. Zigler (Eds.), *Child Abuse: An Agenda For Action*. Oxford University Press.

Bentovim, A., Elton, A., Hildebrand, J., Tranter, M., Vizard, E. (1988). *Sexual Abuse Within the Family*. Bristol: John Wright.

Bentovim, A., Kinston, W. (1991). Focal Family Therapy – joining systems theory with psychodynamic understanding. In A. Gurman and D. Kniskern, *Handbook for Family Therapy Vol II*. New York: Basic Books.

Bentovim, A. (1991). Clinical work with families in which sexual abuse has occurred. In C.R. Hollin and K. Howells (Eds.), *Clinical Approaches to Sex Offenders and Their Victims*. Chichester: Wiley.

Bools, C.N., Neale, B.A., Meadow, S.R. (1991). Co-morbidity associated with fabricated illness (Munchausen Syndrome by Proxy). *Archives of Disease in Childhood*.

Bowlby, J. (1969). *Attachment and Loss Vol I*. Attachment 1969. London: The Hogarth Press.

Bowlby, J.W. (1976). *Attachment and Loss Vol II* – Separation: anxiety and anger. London: Hogarth Press.

Bowlby, J.W. (1980). *Attachment and Loss Vol III* – Loss, sadness and depression. London: Hogarth Press.

Crittenden, P.N., Bonvillian, J.D. (1984). The relationship between maternal risk status and maternal sensitivity. *American Journal of Orthopsychiatry*, **54**, 250–262.

Crittenden, P. (1988). Family and dyadic patterns of functioning in maltreating families. In K. Browne, C. Davies and P. Stratten (Eds.), *Early Prediction and Prevention of Child Abuse*. Chichester: John Wiley.

Egeland, B., Sroufe, A. (1981). Attachment and early maltreatment. *Child Development*, **53**, 44–52.

Finkelhor, D. (1987). The trauma of child sexual abuse: Two models. *Journal of Interpersonal Violence*, **2**, 348–366.

Friedrich, W.N. (1990). *Psychotherapy of sexually abused children and their families*. N.Y.: Norton.

Gaensbauer, T., Sands, K. (1979). Distorted affective communication in abused/ neglected infants and their potential impact on caretakers. *Journal of the American Academy of Child Psychiatry*, **18**, 236–250.

Garbarino, J. (1978). The elusive 'crime' of emotional abuse. In *Child Abuse and Neglect*, **2**, 89–99.

Garland, C. (1991). External disasters and the internal world: An approach to understanding survivors. In J. Holmes (Ed.), *Handbook of Psychotherapy for Psychiatrists*. London: Churchill Livingston.

Gelles, R.J., Strauss, M.A. (1979). Determinants of violence in the family; Toward a theoretical integration. In W.R. Burr, R. Hill, F.I. Nye and I.L. Reiss (Eds.), *Contemporary Theories about the Family*. New York: Free Press.

George, C., Main, M. (1979). Social interactions of young abused children: Approach, avoidance, and aggression. *Child Development*, **50**, 306–318.

Goldstein, J., Freud, A., Solnit, A.J. (1979). *Beyond the Best Interests of the Child*. New York: Free Press.

Goldstein, J., Freud, A., Solnit, A.J. (1979). *Before the Best Interests of the Child*. New York: Free Press.

Goldstein, J., Freud, A., Solnit, A.J., Goldstein, S. (1986). *In the Best Interests of the Child*. New York: Free Press.

Herrenkohl, E.C., Herrenkohl, R.C., Toedter, L., Yanushefsk, A.N. (1984). Parent child interactions in abusive and non-abusive families. *Journal of the American Academy of Child Psychiatry*, **23**, 641–648.

Hodges, J., Tizard, B. (1989). Social and family relationships of ex-institutional adolescents. *Journal of Child Psychology and Psychiatry*, **30**, 77–97.

Jones, D.P.H., Bentovim, A., Cameron, H., Vizard, E., Wolkind, S. (1990). *Child psychiatry and the Children Act 1989*. Presentation to the Judicial Studies Board series of training events 1990–1991, in preparation for the launch of the Children Act.

Kinston, W., Loader, P., Miller, L. (1987). Quantifying the clinical assessment of family health. *Journal of Marital and Family Therapy*, **13**, 49–67.

LaRose, L., Wolfe, D. (1987). Psychological characteristics of parents who abuse or neglect their children. In B.B. Lehey and A.E. Kazdin (Eds.), *Advances in Clinical Child Psychology (Vol X)*. New York: Plemun.

Lask, B., Britten, C., Kroll, L., Magagna, J., Tranter, M. (1991). Children with pervasive refusal. *Archives of Disease in Childhood*, **66**, 866–869.

Lipsett, L. (1983). Stress in infancy: Towards understanding the origins of sleeping behaviour. In N. Garmezy and M. Rutter (Eds.), *Stress, Coping and Development in Children*. New York: McGraw-Hill.

Lynch, M., Roberts, J. (1982). *Consequences of child abuse*. London: Academic Press.

Maccoby, E.E., Martin, J.A. (1983). Socialisation in the context of the family: Parent/child interaction. In E.M. Hetherington (Ed.), *Handbook of Child Psychology (Vol IV, 101–101)*.

McLeer, S., Deblinger, E., Atkins, M., Foa, E., Ralphe, D. (1988). Post Traumatic Disorder in sexually abused children. *Journal American Academy of Child and Adolescent Psychiatry*, **27**, 650–654.

Meadow, R. (1982). Munchausen Syndrome by Proxy and Pseudo-epilepsy. *Archives of Diseases in Childhood*, **57**, 811–812.

Monck, E., Bentovim, A., Goodall, G., Hyde, C., Lwin, R., Sharland, S. (1991). *Child Sexual Abuse: A descriptive and treatment study*. Research report from Institute of Child Health, Hospitals for Sick Children to the Department of Health.

Mullen, P.E., Romans-Clarkson, S., Walton, D.A., Herbison, G.P. (1988). Impact of sexual and physical abuse on women's mental health. *Lancet*, **1648**, 841–845.

Murray, L. (1991). *The effects of maternal depression on future infant development*. Presentation to European Child and Adolescent Psychiatry Conference, London.

Polansky, N.A., Chalmers, M., Buttenweiser, E., Williams, D. (1981). *Damaged Parents: An Anatomy of Child Neglect*. Chicago: University of Chicago Press.

Pynoos, R.S., Eth, S. (1985). (Eds.). *Post-traumatic Stress Disorder in Children*. Los Angeles: American Psychiatric Association.

Rogers, D., Tripp, J., Bentovim, A., Robinson, A., Berry, D., Goulding, R. (1976). Non-accidental poisoning: An extended syndrome of child abuse. *British Medical Journal*, **I**, 793–796.

Rutter, M. (1966). *Children of sick parents – An environmental and psychiatric study*. London: Oxford University Press.

Rutter, M. (1983). Stress, coping, and development: Some issues and some questions. In N. Garmezy and M. Rutter (Eds.), *Stress, Coping and Development in Children*. New York: McGraw-Hill.

Skuse, D. (1991). The relationship between deprivation, physical growth and the impaired development of language. In *Specific Speech and Language Disorders in Children*. London: Whurr. In press.

Spinetta, J.J., Rigler, G. (1972). The child abusing parent: A psychological review. *Psychological Bulletin*, **77**, 296–304.

Terr, L. (1991). Child Trauma: An outline and overview. *American Journal of Psychiatry*, **148**, 10–20.

Tizard, B., Hodges, J. (1978). The effect of early institutional rearing on the development of eight year old children. *Journal of Child Psychology and Psychiatry*, **19**, 99–118.

Wolfe, D.A. (1987). *Child Abuse. Implications for Child Development and Psychopathology.* California: Sage.

The effectiveness of intervention

David P.H. Jones

The intent of this paper is to present information from clinical science which may help both legal decision making and clinicians who plan interventions and give evidence in Court. Under the new Children Act the Court will decide if a child is suffering, or may suffer from significant harm. Then it determines whether to make an order or not, with the child's future welfare as the determining principle. In these considerations the Court has to take into account the Local Authority's plan to help the child and family. Will the proposed intervention achieve improved conditions for the child?

This paper considers what we know about the effectiveness of intervention. Can we treat children and families where abuse and neglect have occurred? We will need to know how likely it is that an individual child will a) be safe and b) have his care (parenting) improved. This information is also likely to be relevant to the making of supervision orders with accompanying conditions, or to their variation and discharge if changes are sought (*Section 39*).

In presenting information from the clinical literature I will avoid the concept of individual dangerousness. Instead I will attempt to consider relevant environmental and personal variables, and their inter-relationships both now and historically. This is necessary because child abuse and neglect has a multi-faceted causation and involves children, their adult carers as well as the family and cultural context in its web. Hence unitary consideration of one person's potential for danger, without appropriate historical and contextual information is relatively valueless.

Studies of families where children have been abused or neglected reveal a proportion who do not respond to the intervention of professionals. Those who work with such families know that some cannot change sufficiently to become safe enough for the child to continue to live there (*Jones, 1987*). Equally a proportion change and provide adequate environments for safe child rearing (if this were not the case all abuse by parents should be sufficient cause for permanent separation of child and parent). In between these extremes practitioners take risks when reuniting (rehabilitating) children and parents.

Practitioners have a considerable body of clinical and research literature available to them, which has examined the outcome of intervention. The following sections summarise our knowledge about the outcome of intervention in child abuse cases, the characteristics of success and failure cases, professional contributions to the success or otherwise of intervention and, finally, discuss the practical implications of all this for our work.

I. Outcome of interventions

a. Methodological aspects

Methodological difficulties have bedeviled child abuse research (*Blythe, 1983; Gough et al, 1988; Smith et al, 1984; Wisdom, 1988*) thereby lowering confidence in research findings. These difficulties include the definitions of abuse used, sampling bias and inadequate specificity about the nature of intervention used and outcome assessment criteria. Definitional problems include: a lack of clear criteria for inclusion in the research, whether abuse reports are accepted at face value, or scrutinised by the researchers, whether, or not, a Court finding of abuse is taken as the index of 'caseness', and whether cases are required to be corroborated legally. Clearly each approach would produce a different sample. Few of the studies have adequately distinguished between the severity of different cases so that, for example, cases of physical abuse involving multiple fractures are lumped together with mild bruising. In several studies, substantiated cases of abuse are included with 'at risk' cases and treated as one group for the purpose of outcome evaluation. Sample size has been a problem in several studies so that conclusions are based on very small numbers of cases. In addition, because the criteria for inclusion are not always specified, the reader is left to guess the representativeness of cases. Cases referred to medical, psychiatric, or psychological centres represent only a minority of the total number of cases of abuse and neglect in an area (*Gough et al, 1988*). Yet many reports have only studied special centres, presumably because such centres have a greater interest in researching their own programmes.

The aims and objectives of the intervention are not always specified and in many studies there is a lack of detail describing exactly what was done, by whom and over what time period. Sometimes it is not clear whether all cases receive the same intervention (usually in the multi-component intervention programmes cases receive varied amounts of the assorted intervention strategies on offer).

A greater emphasis has been placed on outcome measures. Unfortunately outcome measures with such a varied sample of people and interventions can be misleading. Researchers have been criticised for failure to use objective measurements of outcome by employing independent observers. In some studies the instruments used have lacked sensitivity and relevance to the aims of treatment. Gough et al (*1988*) make a well argued case for a shift in emphasis of research strategies towards fully describing the process of intervention, or alternatively focusing on one specific aspect of intervention without attempting to do an outcome study on multi-component large projects, which they deem an impossible task.

The most important outcome variable when assessing efficacy must be the child's condition, but this is often omitted. Important aspects of child health for study include measures of child safety, re-abuse, development, growth and health. Few studies have examined changes in the interaction between parents and children attributable to the intervention (*Wolfe and Bourdeau, 1987*). There has also been criticism of the statistical methods used to determine contribution of different elements of a case to eventual outcome (*Briere, 1988a*).

Despite these difficulties much high quality research has been conducted. As far as practicable, the summaries which follow below have drawn upon those studies which have avoided these major difficulties. Where methodological problems do exist, attention is drawn to this in the text so that the reader can exercise due caution in accepting the findings.

b. Re-abuse

In a significant proportion of cases children are re-abused after intervention or treatment has begun. Despite the fact that reabuse is a key outcome variable, the methods used to assess its frequency have varied from study to study, making comparisons difficult. For example Taw (*1979*) examined social services case records and revealed documentation of re-abuse which was not reflected in official figures and records. Lynch and Roberts (*1982*) found that 20% of the children in their study had been re-abused. To discover this they searched hospital admission records, local authority social services records and individually followed up each of their cases. Other studies have been less exhaustive in their search for evidence of re-abuse. Additionally the length of time over which re-abuse rates are reported has varied from study to study. A further problem has been the fact that re-abuse can mean anything from a slight bruise to a life threatening injury, and very few studies have discriminated between the seriousness of re-abuse (even if they have distinguished between the seriousness of the original injury).

From a clinician's perspective, a re-abuse incident involving slight bruising in an older child is significantly different from skull fracture in an infant. A further fundamental problem has been that re-abuse rates have been quoted for whole samples. However, important issues for clinicians include the timing of re-abuse in relation to reunification attempts, and whether re-abuse occurs by the original abuser or another person. Naturally, those treatment programmes which place emphasis on child placement out of home show lower rates of re-abuse.

The four American demonstration projects (*Cohn and Daro, 1987*) and the description of Project 12 ways (*Lutzker & Rice, 1984*) are useful sources to determine the frequency of re-abuse, as their cases samples are large. Lutzker and Rice (*1984*) compared the re-abuse rate of 352 families who had received services over a five year period with 358 comparable families who were not in their special project. Their re-abuse rate was 21.3%, versus 28.5% for the comparison families, a statistically significant difference. However the re-abuse rate in index families increased over the five years, suggesting that improvement was not maintained.

Additionally there was a possible bias in the project selection criteria, with more motivated families entering the project.

In the first demonstration project there was a 30% re-abuse rate (*see Cohn & Daro, 1987*). The strongest predictor of recidivism was the initial severity of abuse. They compared eleven different programmes and found that the lowest recidivism rates were in the programmes with the greatest proportions of highly trained workers.

Practitioners and Courts are frequently faced with the more severe end of the spectrum of abuse and with weighing up the safety and prospects of an intervention plan. Corby's (*1987*) study of twenty five such cases gives some insight into the expected rate of re-abuse in such a situation, when cases were provided with standard social case work. Seven of the twenty five children were re-abused (28%). Hensey et al (*1983*) studied moderately severe cases of abuse or neglect and found that in the half who were returned home from foster care, the re-abuse rate was 20%. However in this study the nature of the intervention was variable. Cohn and Daro (*1987*) point out that early re-abuse did not always correlate with the final outcome of the case for child and/or parents, suggesting their definition of re-abuse was quite wide, as serious re-abuse would almost certainly have led to child and parent separation.

Reported re-abuse rates within the field of sexual abuse are more difficult to interpret in view of the greater secrecy surrounding sexual abuse. Low rates of re-abuse in incest offenders were reported by Gibbens et al (*1978*), but in this study the offender was often removed from the family in prison, making the comparison with family treatment programmes difficult. Kroth's (*1979*) assessment of Giaretto's programme reported a low re-abuse rate of 0.6%. However, follow-up was short and the rate determined by parent or therapist report, not by children or independent data. By contrast the re-abuse rate in the Great Ormond Street programme was 16% with a further 15% being subject to concern by the researchers (*Bentovim et al, 1988*). In the large demonstration projects (*Cohn & Daro, 1987*), the likelihood of future maltreatment was less in the sexual abuse treatment projects compared with those serving child neglect problems. However these assessments were made by the therapists and cannot be taken as independent judgements.

c. Change during treatment

Examining re-abuse rates has limitations when considering the outcome of intervention. Hence, many studies have tried to examine the extent to which change occurs during intervention. Unfortunately a wide range of dimensions of change have been employed with surprisingly little attention paid to outcomes tapping the quality of life for the abused child. It seems surprising that in the field of child abuse treatment this has not been the central measure, but many studies have dwelt on changes in attitude, belief and knowledge in the parents. The obvious criticism to be levelled at such studies is: what good is a change in such parental factors if it does not result in a) changed behaviour towards the child and b) a better outcome as far as the child is concerned? Studies assessing parental change will only be referred to here if they are linked with child outcome measures, otherwise they are of limited relevance to child abuse treatment planning. As already noted, major methodological problems sometimes affect the strength of the conclusions which can be drawn. Direct comparisons between studies are not necessarily valid, in view of the great variety of designs used. In an attempt to group studies, the large scale studies are considered first, then those conducted in specialised units, followed by those which have focused on more specific research questions within an overall treatment approach.

i. Large scale studies

The demonstration projects showed improvements in the children's developmental status, social and emotional development during the course of treatment (*Cohn & Daro, 1987*). Interestingly the later study (*study 4*) demonstrated gains for over 70% of the young children and adolescents in all functional areas during treatment. This was despite the fact that in that study there were more cases of serious abuse than in the earlier projects. Parents also showed improvements in behaviour and attitude. In approximately half of the cases future abuse was considered unlikely. The provision of group counselling and educational and skill development classes showed a significant relationship to successful outcome. The addition of volunteers to the professional treatment package also improved outcome. As in other studies, (*eg Famularo et al, 1989; Smith &*

Rachman, 1984) many families refused to co-operate and, not surprisingly, those who drop out did not do so well as those remaining in treatment longer than six months (*Cohn and Daro, 1987*). Interestingly, the subgroup of clients who stayed longer than eighteen months did less well (possibly because they included intractable cases where persistence produced little change despite much effort). Better results were achieved by the first demonstration project and by Project 12-ways, where staff made efforts to engage reluctant clients through visits, phone calls and flexible working patterns including home visits (*Cohn, 1979; Cohn & Daro, 1987; Lutzker & Rice, 1984*).

ii. Detailed process studies

These studies have carefully described the process of decision making and the type of case management. Studies of the process whereby typical child protection cases are managed have been less numerous (*see Gough et al, 1988 at Chapter 5*). Gough et al (*1987*) studied all preschool cases which were registered in one area of Scotland. They found that the majority of cases were managed by social workers without much input from health or other agencies. The focus of work was on parenting skills, not on the needs of the child. A very wide variety of predicaments became included in the child abuse 'net'. Poverty and families with marginal coping skills were the commonest cases registered, compared with abuse. To measure outcome in the face of such diversity was therefore very difficult. Nevertheless over half the cases either improved or remained the same. Cases which could be broadly described as neglect did relatively worse than others.

Another approach is to study the management of particular sorts of cases in detail. Corby (*1987*) selected 25 cases from the moderate to severe end of the spectrum of child protection cases. He found great variety in the types of intervention offered, and emphasised the difficulty involved with oversimplifying the concept of outcome.

iii. Specialised centre programmes

There have been several descriptions of specialised programmes which have reported their success or otherwise at achieving change. Elizabeth Elmer and colleagues (1986) report on their results with an intensive programme of treatment, residential assessment, stimulation and parent teaching and modelling, for 'last chance' cases referred by the Courts. They showed significant improvements as far as the children were concerned: height, weight and interaction with their adult carers all improved. However only three of the thirty one children remained at home; the remainder were placed in foster care (Elmer et al, 1986). Lynch and Roberts (1982) report that nine out of thirty nine children (23%) they studied did well over the follow up period. The remainder had continuing problems to varying degrees. In thirteen of the thirty three children who were not in care, but still at home, child care was poor. These children frequently had accompanying medical, psychological and school problems.

iv. Focused studies

These include most of the behavioral modification programmes as well as a small number of studies which have used other treatment modalities. In general, the outcome assessment has not encompassed the whole process of child and family change. Rather it has focused on one aspect of change in order to see whether the specific aims of treatment have been met. For example, Nicol et al, (1988) compared a focused case work approach based on Paterson's social learning theory, and aimed at parent child interactions, with structured play therapy for the child alone. The groups were well matched and both sets of families continued to have normal social case work and child protection services. There was a high drop out rate in both groups, but greater improvement was seen in the focused case work regime: this led to a specific reduction in coercive and negative behaviour.

Kitchur and Bell (1989) described their group treatment for pre-adolescent, sexually abused girls utilising self esteem and child behaviour outcome measures and demonstrated the benefit of the group in both these dimensions, in a methodologically sound study. Deblinger et al (1990) studied a group of children treated with a cognitive behavioral programme specifically designed for child victims of sexual abuse. Using standardised measures they demonstrated significant improvement in both the child and their non offending parent. Studies such as these which focus on a specific aspect of an overall treatment plan for abused children and families are of great value to practitioners who are developing treatment plans.

II. Characteristics of successful and failure cases

This section of the paper will describe those studies which have described the characteristics of children and/or families where intervention was successful or, alternatively, unsuccessful. Studies concentrating on this aspect of outcome have identified several characteristics which describe families falling into these two extremes of the spectrum of outcome. Studies have not distinguished the relative weight of each characteristic, so far, and so to state which factors are the most important is not yet possible. However, the factors listed below appear in more than one study describing the unsuccessful cases, lending credence to their inclusion below. Therefore, the weighting of different factors in an individual case must remain, by necessity, a clinical decision.

- Continuing parental denial of abuse or impairment

- Parents who refuse help or do not cooperate with professional help. (Clinically refusal is seen more frequently but not exclusively in cases of burning, scalding, Munchausen Syndrome by Proxy (MSBP) and severe sexual abuse.)

- Severe parental personality problems: antisocial, aggressive or inadequate

- Parental mental handicap with accompanying mental illness

- Persistent parental substance/alcohol misuse

- Parental psychosis with delusions involving the child.

- Severe accompanying child neglect or psychological abuse. (Included here are cases where parents demonstrate pervasive lack of empathy for the child.)

- Severe sexual abuse (involving penetration and of long duration).

- Sadistic abuse or that which includes slow premeditated infliction of pain and suffering.

- Mixed abuse cases

- Certain types of abuse cases, eg MSBP, deliberate poisoning, scalding and burns.

A further problem is that there is circularity of reasoning involved with these studies. That is, the decision is made by practitioners not to proceed with treatment because of certain factors which are, in turn, listed as the characteristics of 'untreatable' cases. Hence the studies describe current practice.

The studies which have been conducted do have several other methodological problems, too. One issue is that there has been a lack of distinction between cases where parents refuse to even start treatment, those who engage initially but then do not cooperate later, and finally those who start and cooperate but cannot change enough or sufficiently quickly for their child's development. These are vital distinctions which are not clear in the studies. This issue is complicated by the unrepresentativeness of cases. As Gough et al (*1988*) point out, studies less commonly describe all cases in an area, concentrating instead on specialised treatment centres which select cases for inclusion. Despite these cautions some of the findings from selected studies will now be discussed.

Early studies describing treatment failures concentrated on personality attributes or psychiatric descriptions of the parents (*Kempe and Kempe, 1978; Gabinet, 1983; Green et al, 1981*). These studies were not able to relate such parental qualities to severity of type of initial abuse, parent-child interaction, family functioning, quality and type of treatment or indeed child variables. Despite these methodological reservations, their descriptions of intervention and failures show some common threads. The Kempes (*1978*) pointed to seven groups of parents who commonly proved untreatable: aggressive psychopaths, parents with delusions that involve their child, cruel sadistic parents who painfully abuse their children with pre-meditation, extreme fanatics, drug and substance abusers, mentally handicapped parents, and families with a history of prior serious injury or child abuse death. Gabinet (*1983*) found that parents who are sociopaths, addicts, severely inadequate personalities, mentally handicapped combined with a personality disorder and focal abusers were over represented in her treatment failure cases. (Focal abusers were those who did not have problems in areas other than abusing their children, and were similar to some of the Kempes' fanatics, who were outwardly respectable yet parented their children abusively). In Gabinet's study severely mentally handicapped or psychotic parents were not accepted for treatment. However, the other major group in her study who proved untreatable were those who refused treatment.

Green et al (1981) found that treatment failures were more likely to have the following characteristics: to have repeatedly abused their child prior to discovery, to be involuntarily in treatment, to have ended treatment prematurely against advice, to deny that they had abused their child, to have a history of serious abuse in childhood themselves, to have had premature expectations of their child and to show an impaired ability to relate to other adults. In a later study of forty five abusive parents from the same treatment centre, Ferleger et al (1988) found that lack of compliance by parents was the best indicator of later re-abuse (which occurred in 40% of their sample). Famularo et al (1988) looked at parental compliance in more detail and discovered that it was lower in those cases involving physical abuse and sexual abuse, than in neglect, and was substantially reduced if there was parental substance abuse.

One of the biggest problems facing those providing intervention services in abuse and neglect is that of overcoming high refusal rates and parental denial that a problem exists at all. One controversial aspect of this is the extent to which civil court orders help to motivate reluctant parents where abuse has been substantiated in courts. Wolfe et al's (1980) randomised prospective trial of court order versus voluntary treatment provided some preliminary evidence that the court ordered group did better than the voluntary. This was despite the fact that the court ordered group tended to contain cases of greater severity. In a similar vein Irueste-Montes and Montes (1988) looked at thirty five court ordered cases of abuse and neglect compared with thirty who entered treatment voluntarily. There was a high drop out rate from both groups and once again the court ordered group seemed to contain the more serious cases of abuse. Their outcome measures included a careful observation of the quality of interactions between parent and child. Both groups improved to an equal degree in terms of parent/child interactions. The authors interpret the results as indicating that court orders do not act as an obstruction to effective intervention. Bearing in mind that in both studies the Court ordered group contained more serious cases, yet still did as well or better than the voluntary, these studies support clinical impression that coercion helps improve outcome.

In this country Dale et al (*1986*) described the experience of the NSPCC Special Unit in Rochdale, working with the serious end of the spectrum of child abuse cases; they had twenty six families in all. Their intervention consisted of a three to four month intensive assessment of the capacity for change followed by continuing rehabilitative efforts over the next two years. 55% of the children were included in their 'sustained rehabilitation' group (ie the group with whom they continued rehabilitative efforts after the end of the intensive assessment period). They had therefore weeded out the families who would not comply with their treatment programme and those with whom rehabilitation was attempted but proved unsafe or not possible. In the 55% who remained in their 'sustained rehabilitation' group there was no re-abuse. Independent outcome measures were not employed but their study contains a wealth of valuable detail about clinical decision making and the range of their work with children and families.

The 'sustained rehabilitation' group were characterised by parents who took greater responsibility for the abuse caused; showed an awareness of difficulties in the spousal relationship and their parenting ability; and demonstrated a willingness to tackle the difficulties. In addition the children demonstrated a wish, either directly or indirectly, to return home. By contrast in the group where permanent separation, voluntary or otherwise, was the end result, the parents did not take responsibility for the abuse caused; frequently failed to engage with the therapeutic staff; and themselves tended to have a history of severe abuse and/or deprivation in their own childhoods, which they were unprepared to tackle during therapeutic work. With regard to their own adult partnership, they lacked awareness of difficulties or there was continuing violence between them. In addition they found that the permanent separation group were associated with the more serious injuries. By more serious they include more extreme forms of violence and resultant injury together with those where there was premeditation or sadism involved (eg burning, scalding). This association between outcome and seriousness was not found by the Denver Circle House Group (*McBogg et al, 1979*) or the Park Hospital Group (*Lynch and Roberts, 1982*). However definitions of seriousness were not necessarily comparable and sample size and range of seriousness makes comparison unreliable.

The final end point of decision making in the American Civil Courts is that of the termination of parental rights, after a treatment plan has been tried and failed. Schetky et al (*1979*) report their experience when assessing such families prior to termination of parental rights hearings. They report that parental lack of empathy, viewing the child as a possession, parental history of abuse in childhood with current low self esteem, poor judgement and impulsivity, maternal psychosis and paternal personality disorders (usually sociopathy) were the most common features among those parents whose rights were terminated. The authors add that many of these parents refused any form of help or treatment in the first place.

Does the type or severity of abuse correlate with treatment outcome? These are more complex issues than appear at first sight. The discrimination between types of abuse has been poorly distinguished in most studies. Practitioners tend to select what they perceive as the most prominent category when filling out statistical returns, frequently ignoring mixed categories or coding of abuse type. A further complication is that abuse type itself is an administrative label, to a large degree, and not an accurate description for all the abuses and neglects befalling an individual child.

As clinicians, we have stressed the need for a more complete understanding of the range of abuse and neglect and parenting qualities in any individual abuse case (*Bentovim, 1990; Jones, 1991; Jones & Alexander, 1987*). Does neglect or emotional abuse accompany the abuse, and if so to what extent? One recent study has underlined the concerns of clinicians that underlying emotional abuse and neglect may be as important, if not more so, than the officially categorised abuse type, in terms of eventual outcome for the child (*Claussen & Crittenden, 1991*). None of the treatment outcome studies have documented adequately the full range of abuse and neglect present in individual cases, let alone related this to outcome in order to overcome such issues (Claussen & Crittenden being one of the first to attempt to do so). Interestingly, Claussen and Crittenden (*1991*) found that child outcome was unrelated to severity of original injury, whereas physical abuse coexisting with psychological maltreatment was highly correlated with outcome. Also physical abuse hardly ever occurred without concurrent psychological maltreatment. By contrast, psychological abuse did occur alone. Thus the occurrence of mixed types of abuse and severe underlying emotional abuse and neglect is highly likely to affect outcome and response to treatment.

'Severity' itself is a complex notion. It is likely to include the degree and extent of physical harm, duration and frequency of abuse. Still further factors appear to include the extent of premeditation (*Dale et al, 1986*), degree of threat and coercion (*Conte & Schuerman, 1987*) sadism (*Dale et al, 1986*), and bizarre or unusual elements in child sexual abuse (*Briere, 1988b*). Each of these, or combinations thereof have been associated with more severe effects on the child and/or relatively greater difficulty for treatment. It must be noted that, at least in part, severity is defined by outcome and hence the issues of severity and successful outcome are partially circular constructs.

In summary then, there have been variable findings with respect to type of abuse and outcome. It seems that mixed types of abuse and severe types of sexual abuse may be very resistant to treatment. Also there are few, if any, case reports of successful intervention in Munchausen syndrome by proxy, or deliberate poisoning cases. With regard to severity, although this is a complex concept, there is an association between severity of abuse and treatment outcome, in some, but not all, studies.

One study has attempted to examine the relative contribution of these different factors. Ferleger et al (*1988*) showed a significant interaction between re-abuse and severity of abuse, in relation to percentage of kept appointments, suggesting that the relationship between severe abuse and outcome is not a direct one, but one which involves the degree to which parents can engage with treatment efforts. This emphasises the critical position of compliance in child abuse work (see above).

Studies of successful families have been less numerous but are of equal relevance to practising clinicians. Lynch and Roberts (*1982*) described in detail the nine out of thirty nine children who did well in their study; they featured: uncomplicated pregnancy and birth, no prematurity, younger age (less than two years) when diagnosed, higher levels of language and intellectual abilities, absence of brain damage, and fewer subsequent placements. Conte and Scheurman (*1987*) demonstrated that, in sexual abuse cases, children who did well were more likely to have been subjected to sexual abuse which was non-penetrative, to have received the support of an adult person in the wake of discovery of abuse, and to have developed more healthy and appropriate attributions about who was responsible for their abuse. Follow up studies of abused (*Egeland et al, 1988*) and deprived (*Rutter, 1989*) women, currently parenting their own children, have under-scored the importance of corrective school experiences, non-abusive and corrective relationships with peers during childhood, having a non abusive adult partner who provides support, and therapeutic intervention as a child, as important factors distinguishing women who parent their own offspring satisfactorily, despite their miserable childhood experiences.

III. Professional factors

The unwillingness of a significant minority of parents to comply with the professionals' management plan is a central theme in several studies (*Gabinet, 1983; Smith & Rachman, 1984*). Some families do not choose to engage at all, others seem to try but drop out of treatment early on. Not surprisingly, this group have been poorly studied as they tend to be unavailable to researchers too. But what about the professional contribution to the professional/client relationship? In general, very little work has examined critically the work of the professional system. There is a large literature describing the factors which professionals take into account when making decisions (*see helpful summary by Dalgleish and Drew, 1989*) but much less interest in how professionals intervene and what consumers think about intervention.

Corby (*1987*) and Brown (*1984*) have demonstrated that how professionals intervene may be relatively more important to parents than exactly what they do. Consumers (parents) found patronising and authoritarian approaches with inadequate explanation the most difficult and negative professional responses. Both studies found that negative initial experiences influence parents future relationships with the professionals. On the other hand, parents responded warmly to empathic accessible professionals who emanated genuineness and a positive regard for them, despite the use of child protection powers. In Brown's study (*1984*) families often expressed the wish to have a different social worker from the one they were allocated, complaining that they could not get on with him/her. In general the professional response to this request is to minimise its relevance, taking it as a further demonstration of the parent's oppositionalism and lack of compliance. At present a lack of available resources make such choices a luxury. However, it should be noted that those who can afford to pay for therapeutic help are able to exercise some choice over whom they work with concerning sensitive personal issues. By contrast, social services clients are rarely permitted to exercise choice over which professional they work with (*Brown, 1984*). Increasingly, agencies have been attempting to provide choice, wherever practicable. However, this question has not been systematically explored, to date.

IV. Practical implications

How can all this material be incorporated into the management of cases where there has been child abuse? Are there sufficiently robust findings from more than one study to enable us to have confidence in the research findings to date? While further research is almost always needed in such complex matters, certain lessons can already be usefully drawn and applied to help the practitioner. Initially, the task for professionals is investigation to determine whether abuse or neglect has occurred. Following this, the next stage in the assessment process, once abuse or neglect has been established, is to assess the child and family context sufficiently to be able to secure child protection. Later on, the process develops into an assessment of the likelihood of change. Looked at in this way, assessment continues throughout intervention. There is good reason to suggest that the quality of the work in the investigation phase sets the tone for subsequent interventions. Some parents may be unable to engage in any form of change at all, even at this very early stage.

The Department of Health (*1988*) considers the comprehensive assessment should follow by about a week or more, the initial investigation phase. They consider that anything up to 3 months may be taken in conducting this assessment, particularly in the more difficult cases. In addition to the professionals' immediate cause for concern (abuse or neglect etc.), 9 areas are recommended for examination by the professional when conducting such assessment (*Table 1*). This list of domains to be explored is complimentary in scope to that of a child psychiatric or psychological assessment (*Jones, 1991*). The latter is likely to place greater emphasis on the developmental perspective and on the presence or absence of attachment problems and psychiatric disorder. Both assessment approaches stress the importance of examining the positive and negative features of each case (*Jones, 1991*).

Table 1

Comprehensive assessment

The causes for concern
The child
Family composition
Individual profile of parents/carers
Couple relationship
Family interactions
Networks
Financial factors
Physical conditions

(*Department of Health, 1988*)

The research findings can be summarised in a table of those characteristics which have been associated with a more positive outcome, contrasted with those associated with a more negative one (*Table 2*). While no factor should be taken as a definite indicator that a particular child and

Factors involved in success or failure

Factors	Rehabilitation more likely to fail	Rehabilitation more likely to succeed

Parental	Personality – Antisocial
	           – Sadism
	           – Aggressive
		Non-abusive partner

	Lack of compliance Denial of problems Substance abuse/ alcoholism Paranoid psychosis Abuse in childhood – not recognised as a problem	Compliance Acceptance of problem
Parenting and parent/child interaction	Disordered attachment Lack of empathy for child Own needs before child	Normal attachment Empathy for child
Abuse factors	Severe PA* – severe damage: Burns/scalds Severe FTT Mixed abuse CSA with penetration and of long duration MSBP Sadistic abuse	If severe, yet compliance and lack of denial, success still possible Less severe forms of abuse
Child factors	Developmental delay with special needs V. young – requiring rapid parental change	Healthy child attributions (in CSA) Later age of onset One good corrective relationship
Professional factors	Lack of resources Ineptitude	Therapeutic relationship with child Outreach to family Partnership with parents
Social setting	Social isolation	More local child care facilities Volunteer networks

*Key to abbreviations
PA   = Physical abuse
FTT   = Failure to thrive
MSBP   = Munchausen Syndrome by Proxy
CSA   = Child sexual abuse

and family will not be amenable to treatment, or on the other hand will definitely respond, the characteristics listed may alert the practitioner to positive or negative features about the individual case which aid planning. In the clinical situation these various factors will need to be weighed relative to one another. These case factors will now need to be considered in the light of the parents' likely compliance. Applying these research findings to the individual case will allow a prognosis to be estimated. Cases with a poorer prognosis are more likely to need comprehensive court powers to secure the child's safety. Those with a good prognosis may not require an order at all, despite perhaps the presence of significant harm. In between these extremes lie many cases where the estimated prognosis is guarded or qualified. In these, some order may be necessary to provide the necessary catalyst and/or framework for continuing assessment and therapy.

Gauging parental compliance can prove difficult because the parent may be under pressure from extended family, solicitors or through personal guilt, to appear more cooperative than she or he truly feels. Under the new Children Act, the wide menu of available Orders together with the variation which can be sought in some Orders (eg the new Supervision Order, Interim Orders with directions), will allow for subsequent changes to be made if parental co-operation is insufficiently sustained.

Professional factors will also need to be considered, including the availability of basic resources. From this matrix the professional can specify a process of change for the family involved. This may include any treatment provision, proposed interventions, counselling and support. If relevant, the stages which the family are expected to undergo may be specified. Increasingly, practitioners find it useful to set out the criteria for gauging whether the intervention will have been successful or otherwise, at this initial planning stage (*Jones, 1991*). Lastly, but probably all importantly, the time scale for intervention will need to be set out at the

Table 3

Considerations when estimating prospects for change

Case and professional factors (Table 2)

Expected process of change (inc. treatment, counselling)

Criteria for success

Timescale for change

beginning. This is because the time scale will depend on the age and developmental needs of the individual child. Table 3 lists the processes which may be involved in estimating the prospects for a change after a comprehensive assessment has been undertaken. In some cases an initial assessment will be necessary, followed by a clinical review and a setting of further goals for intervention, especially in complicated cases. Other cases, however, may be able to be dealt with in a single process of assessment, goal setting, followed by assessment of outcome in the future.

How might these assessments be conducted under the new Act? It might be said that the Act's guiding principle of avoiding delay will result in insufficient time being available to conduct complex assessments. However, the menu of available orders, the significantly strengthened new supervision order, together with the opportunities available under the new Act to bring cases back to court, should mean that even complex cases can be comprehensively assessed within a time scale which ensures that the necessary work is not compromised.

Conclusions

The available research can aid clinical decision making. The research on the outcome of intervention in child abuse engenders realism about the general likelihood of success. However, given that severe child abuse by a caregiver represents such a severe breakdown in parenting, it is hardly surprising that treatment results are modest. Above all, the results of these studies provide a powerful case for careful treatment planning. Such planning includes specifying the aims and objectives of intervention, the criteria for success or failure and the expected time frame, given the child's developmental status, right at the start of intervention. Cases take time to assess properly as well as to effect change. Intervention may need to be planned in stages. The legal umbrella necessary for each stage may prove different as the case unfolds, dependent upon progress and parental cooperativeness. Professionals working with abusing families need to appreciate the research messages in order to plan interventions. Also, once professionals appreciate that success rates are modest, it becomes clear that the important 'outcome' to measure must be the welfare of the child.

In some cases hard decisions will need to be made swiftly enough to prevent the child's development being adversely affected. Family rehabilitation is desirable, but only provided that an improved situation for the child is the paramount aim of any intervention. Wald (*1982*) proposed an outside time limit of 12 months for those families in which the child is under 3 years, and 18 months for those over 3 years, before permanent alternative plans for parenting are sought. Professionals can be encouraged to regard effective relinquishment as an equally legitimate therapeutic goal in some cases. This position becomes perfectly acceptable, if 'success' is seen as essentially a child welfare criterion. Furthermore, in order to prevent 'burn-out' and to preserve human and financial resources, we cannot afford to keep trying relentlessly with cases where there is minimal hope of change. This constitutes a realistic acceptance of both our own and the families' limitations, preserving therapeutic optimism for the more feasible cases.

Bibliography

Bentovim, A. (1990). Family Violence: Clinical Aspects (Section VII, Chapter 8, pp 543–561). In R. Bluglass and P. Bowden (Eds.), *Principles and Practice of Forensic Psychiatry*. Edinburgh: Churchill Livingstone.

Bentovim, A., Elton, A., Hildebrand, J., Tranter, M., Vizard, E. (1988). *Child Abuse Within the Family: Assessment and Treatment*. London: John Wright.

Blythe, B. (1983). A critique of outcome evaluation in child abuse treatment. *Child Welfare*, **62**: 325–335.

Briere, J. (1988a). Controlling for family variables in abuse effects research: a critique of the partialling approach. *J Interpers Violence* **3**: 80–89.

Briere, J. (1988b). The long term clinical correlates of childhood sexual victimisation. *Annals of the New York Academy of Science*, **528**: 327–334.

Brown, C. (1984). *Child Abuse Parents Speaking*. Bristol: University of Bristol.

Claussen, A.H., Crittenden, P.M. (1991). Physical and psychological maltreatment, relations among types of maltreatment. *Child Abuse & Neglect* **15**: 5–18.

Cohn, A.H. (1979). Effective treatment of child abuse and neglect. *Social Work* **24**: 513–519.

Cohn, A.H., Daro, D. (1987). Is treatment too late; what 10 years of evaluative research tells us. *Child Abuse & Neglect* **11**: 433–442.

Conte, J.R., Schuerman, J.R. (1987). Factors associated with an increased impact of sexual abuse. *Child Abuse & Neglect* **11**: 201–212.

Corby, B. (1987). *Working With Child Abuse*. Oxford: Oxford University Press.

Dale, P., Davies, M., Morrison, T., Waters, J. (1986). *Dangerous Families; Assessment and Treatment of Child Abuse*. London: Tavistock Publications.

Dalgleish, L., Drew, E. (1989). The relationship of child abuse indicators to the assessment of perceived risk and to the court's decision to separate. *Child Abuse & Neglect* **13**: 491–506.

Deblinger, E., McVeer, S.V., Henry, D. (1990). Cognitive behavioural treatment for sexually abused children suffering post traumatic stress; preliminary findings. *Journal of the American Academy of Child & Adolescent Psychiatry* **29**: 747–752.

Department of Health. (1988). *Protecting Children, a Guide for Social Workers Undertaking a Comprehensive Assessment*. London: Her Majesty's Stationery Office.

Egeland, B., Jacobvitz, D., Sroufe, L.A. (1988). Breaking the cycle of abuse. *Child Development* **59**: 1080–1088.

Elmer, E. (1986). Outcome of residential treatment for abused and high risk infants. *Child Abuse & Neglect* **10**: 351–360.

Famularo, R., Kinscherff, R., Bunshaft, D., Spivak, Fenton, T. (1989). Parental compliance to court ordered treatment interventions in cases of child maltreatment. *Child Abuse & Neglect* **13**: 507–514.

Ferleger, N., Glenwick, D., Gaines, R., Green, A.H. (1988). Identifying correlates of re-abuse in maltreating parents. *Child Abuse & Neglect* **12**: 41–49.

Gabinet, L. (1983). Child abuse treatment failures reveal need for redefinition of the problem. *Child Abuse & Neglect* **7**: 395–402.

Gibbens, T.C.N., Soothill, K.L., Way, C.K. (1978). Sibling and parent–child incest offenders. *British Journal of Criminology* **18**: 40–52.

Gough, D.A., Boddy, F.A., Dunning, N., Stone, P.H. (1987) *A Longitudinal Study of Child Abuse in Glasgow, Volume 1*. Glasgow: Public Health Research Unit, The University of Glasgow.

Gough, D.A., Taylor J.P., Boddy, F.A. (1988). *Child Abuse Interventions, a Review of the Research Literature*. Final Report to the Department of Health, London. (Available from Public Health Research Unit, The University of Glasgow.)

Green, A.H., Power, E., Steinbook, B., Gaines, R. (1981). Factors associated with successful and unsuccessful intervention with child abusive families. *Child Abuse & Neglect* **5**: 45–52.

Hensey, O.J., Williams, J., Rosenbloom, L. (1983). Intervention in child abuse, experience in Liverpool. *Developmental Medicine and Child Neurology* **25**: 606–611.

Irueste-Montes, A., Montes, F. (1988). Court ordered vs. voluntary treatment of abusive and neglectful parents. *Child Abuse & Neglect* **12**: 33–39.

Jones, D.P.H. (1987). The untreatable family. *Child Abuse & Neglect* **11**: 409–420.

Jones, D.P.H. (1991). Working with the Children Act: tasks and responsibilities of the child and adolescent psychiatrist. In C. Lindsey (Ed.), *Proceedings of the Children Act 1989 Course*. London: Royal College of Psychiatrists. Occasional Paper Series.

Jones, D.P.H., Alexander, H. (1987). Treating the abusive family within the family care system. In R. Helfer and R.S. Kempe (Eds.), *The Battered Child*, 4th edition. London: University of Chicago Press.

Kempe, R.S., Kempe, C.H. (1978). The untreatable family. In *Child Abuse*. London: Open Books: pp 128–131.

Kitchur, M., Bell, R. (1989). Group psychotherapy with pre-adolescent sex abuse victims, literature review and a description of an inner city group. *International Journal of Group Psychotherapy* **39**: 285–310.

Kroth, J.A. (1979). Family therapy impact on intrafamilial child sexual abuse. *Child Abuse and Neglect* **3**: 297–302.

Lutzker, J.R., Rice, J.M. (1984). Project Twelve Ways, measuring outcome of a large in-home service for treatment and prevention of child abuse and neglect. *Child Abuse & Neglect* **8**: 519–524.

Lynch, M.A., Roberts, J. (1982). *Consequences of Child Abuse*. London: Academic Press.

McBogg, P., McQuiston, M., Alexander, H. (1979). Circle House residential treatment programme. *Child Abuse & Neglect* **3**: 863–867.

Nicol, A.R., Smith, J., Kay, B., Hall, D., Barlow, J., Williams, B. (1988). A focused casework approach to the treatment of child abuse: a controlled comparison. *J Child Psychol Psychiatry* **29**: 703–711.

Rutter, M. (1989). Intergenerational continuities and discontinuities in serious parenting difficulties. In D. Cicchetti and V. Carlson (Eds.), *Child Maltreatment, Theory and Research on the Causes and Consequences of Child Abuse and Neglect*. Cambridge: Cambridge University Press.

Schetky, D.H., Angell, R., Morrison, C.V., Sack, W.H. (1979). A study of 51 cases of termination of parental rights. *Journal of the American Academy of Child Psychiatry* **18**: 366–383.

Smith, J.E., Rachman, S.J. (1984). Non-accidental injury to children: II. A controlled evaluation of a behavioural management programme. *Behaviour Research and Therapy* **22**: 349–366.

Smith, J.E., Rachman, S.J., Yule, B. (1984). Non-accidental injury to children: III. Methodological problems of evaluative treatment research. *Behaviour Research and Therapy* **22**: 367–383.

Taw, T.E. (1979). The issue of reinjury: An agency experience. *Child Abuse & Neglect* **3**: 591–600.

Wald, M.S. (1982). State intervention on behalf of endangered children. *Child Abuse & Neglect* **9**: 3–45.

Wisdom, K. (1988). Sampling biases and implications for child abuse research. *American Journal of Ortho Psychiatry* **58**: 260–270.

Wolfe, D.A., Bourdeau, P.A. (1987). Current issues in the assessment of abusive and neglectful parent–child relationships. *Behav Assess* **9**: 271–290.

Wolfe, D.A., Aragona, J., Kaufman, K., Sandler, J. (1980). The importance of adjudication in the treatment of child abusers: Some preliminary findings. *Child Abuse & Neglect* **4**: 127–135.

Change, control and the legal framework

Tony Morrison

The purpose of this chapter is to assist practitioners in thinking through the difficult issues associated with decisions about the use of Supervision, Care and Section 8 Orders in child protection cases. The focus is on the use of orders which have a therapeutic, as well as protective purpose. This distinguishes them from Emergency Protection Orders which have a purely investigative/protective purpose. The aim of the paper is to analyse the relationship between control, as represented by the making of an order, and change.

The chapter addresses four areas:

The principles which should underpin the use of Supervision or Care Orders;

How abusing families change, and who is treatable;

The relationship between compulsion and change;

When orders may be necessary.

Philosophy of the Children Act: principles of intervention

This comprehensive piece of legislation is underpinned by a number of fundamental principles which are an attempt to resolve one of the most enduring questions in child protection work, the balance between family autonomy, and state intervention to protect children. Child abuse enquiries remind us forcibly that one of the most difficult issues in social work practice remains that of how social workers operate the control and power essential to the effective exercise of their protective duties. Either we are accused of doing too little, too late, or of doing too much, too soon.

While it is social workers who are scapegoated for this compromise, we must recognise that the roots of such problems lie in societal, and thus, governmental, attitudes to children and families. As Alice Miller (*1983*) writes, commenting about western society's attitudes to children "We are still barely conscious of how harmful it is to treat children in a degrading manner. Treating them with respect and recognising the consequences of their being humiliated are, by no means, intellectual matters, otherwise their importance would long since have been generally realised. To empathise with what a child is feeling when he or she is defenceless, hurt, or humiliated, is like suddenly seeing in a mirror the suffering of one's own childhood, something many people must ward off out of fear ... we ward it off with the aid of illusions, such as, for example, believing that children were mistreated in previous centuries, or are so in distant countries or cultures".

The degree to which the Children Act succeeds in reflecting or resolving the tensions between the rights of families and the needs of children will be critical, Upon this will depend the degree to which social workers will be able to practice with more confidence, and less ambivalence, in protecting and caring for abused children.

Section 1 of the Children Act sets out the welfare principle. The welfare of the child is paramount, and delay is considered prejudicial to the child's interests. No orders are to be made unless the court considers that it is better for the child to make an order than to make no order at all. This has been expressed as the principle of 'judicial non-interference'. White, Carr and Lowe (*1990*) comment in their guide to the Act "authorities must develop co-operative strategies to work with parents to resolve their problems. The Act provides for doing what is reasonable or working with parents by agreement. If no agreement can be reached, the authority will have to consider seeking compulsory powers".

Local authorities will have to demonstrate in detail why voluntary collaboration is not, or is no longer, possible, and exactly how an order will make the situation better for the child. It will not be sufficient to talk about the need for an order just in terms of protection. The presentation of such court cases will, thus, require a far higher standard of early and well coordinated inter-agency case planning. Such planning will, in turn, need to be based on a shared understanding between agencies of how change occurs and the place of statutory intervention within the change process.

The over-riding ethos of the Act is clear. Families must be supported, and only intruded upon in the most severe cases. Services must be delivered on a voluntary basis wherever possible and the goal should be to work in partnership with parents.

The question of how this will fit with the professional and political imperative to protect children is not an easy one to answer. The Department of Health's Introductory Guide to the Act (*1989*) acknowledges that a deliberate tension exists within the Act between the welfare principle and the principle of parental responsibility. Eekelaar (*1990*) points out that "parental responsibility needs to be seen and understood in the context of a general conservative belief in the desirability of privatising the responsibility for the care of dependent individuals, including children, and the diminution of the role of the state". Bainham (*1990*) makes the point even more clearly when he concludes "the dominant ethos of the legislation is the supremacy of parental preferences, and the identification of the welfare of children with these. It is argued that parents themselves are subject to the legal limitations of the welfare principle, that is that they are required in law to exercise their responsibility in the best interests of children. I have argued elsewhere that without external superintendence or control, this is a meaningless restraint on parental power. The welfare principle has, in reality, been hi-jacked by non-interventionism". Children must be protected whilst, at the same time, family life must be preserved.

How do abusing families change?

Before looking at the relationship between compulsion and change, it is important to review what is known about the treatment of abusing families. Such knowledge is crucial in assessing the need for a court order.

Different large scale evaluations of American treatment programmes by Cohn and Daro (*1987*), Dubovitz (*1990*), and Kolko (*1987*) have come to the following conclusions which are summarised here.

a. Clients involved in treatment for less than six months, or over 18 months, were less likely to make progress.

b. Progress was greater with a comprehensive package of services dealing with both the concrete and inter-personal needs of family members.

c. Family therapy, groupwork, and parent skill classes were all seen as more effective than individual work.

d. Lay therapy was effective with motivated clients.

e. The projects that were most successful in protecting the child, separated the child from the abuser.

f. Re-abuse rates during treatment were between 30 and 47%.

g. The prognosis for change in cases of sexual abuse was much better than for neglect, or severe physical abuse or emotional abuse.

h. Packages of direct services to children were effective in ameliorating their disturbance.

i. Specific treatments work best when they are targeted at specific problems.

Are all families treatable?

The notion of non-treatability is not an easy one for us to accept as it may serve to undermine the optimism which is so necessary for our work with families who are often deprived and sometimes disturbed. David Jones (*1987*) has pointed out that "the idea that some families do not respond, appears to be anathema to some practitioners and researchers alike. ... in some quarters, to determine that a family is untreatable, is unacceptable". Nonetheless, there is clear evidence from research that we have to face the fact that a significant proportion of parents who abuse children are likely to be untreatable.

Cohn & Daro (*ibid*) in their review of 89 programmes quote Kempe as estimating that "regardless of treatment used, 20% of parents will be treatment failures, leading to the child not returning home. 40% of parents will change and grow on a permanent basis, and 40% of parents will not physically re-abuse, but will continue to emotionally harm their children". This corresponds with the findings of Bentovim et al (*1987*) in treating cases of sexual abuse, who concluded that 35% of their sample remained unchanged or worse, following treatment.

Jones (*1987*) summarises factors associated with untreatable families. The major factors are parental denial of responsibility for the abuse, lack of empathy for the child, personality disorder, sadistic or very serious abuse, and refusal to accept help. In a climate of increasing demands and decreasing resources it is inevitable that cost benefit analysis will play an increasing part in decision making with such families. We will need to assess more quickly who is treatable.

What is the relationship between compulsion and change?

Two important American studies have looked at the significance of court adjudication in treating abusing families. Famularo et al. (*1989*) studied 136 child abuse cases in which children were transferred from parental to state guardianship, looking at treatment outcomes for a variety of court ordered treatment programmes. "The results clearly show that court involvement and subsequent risk of loss of custody of their children alone, do not have the effect of motivating many parents to participate in court ordered interventions ... In cases that involve parental substance abuse, and/or the more severe forms of child maltreatment, the court and involved agencies need to give scrupulous attention to the child protective aspects of the case, perhaps including removing 'at risk' children from the parents, at least until compliance with court orders and subsequent assessment of risk can be evaluated." In other words, even with compulsion some parents will remain untreatable. For the children involved in such cases the need for court orders to protect their futures is essential.

An early study by Wolfe et al (*1980*) examined the effect of court adjudication in referrals to a behaviourally orientated child management programme. This study concluded "that those parents who refused treatment were those who had no strong contingencies to motivate their initial participation. On the other hand, those parents who had little choice but to comply with the court order, began the process of change. The data suggests that a court ordered family is approximately five times more likely to complete treatment successfully than a voluntary family. Similarly, a voluntary family is approximately five times more likely to refuse treatment than a court ordered family ... It appears that judicial support is a necessary component to treatment."

Despite the paucity of available research on the use of court ordered treatment, models of UK practice have been described in which the overt use of statutory control has been seen as having a positive effect on the process of change with abusing families. In particular, the work of the Marlborough Family Service in London and that of the NSPCC team in Rochdale are examples. Both worked with families in which children had been seriously physically abused or neglected, or sexually abused.

Asen et al (*1989*) noted "In many cases there is considerable resistance and often overt denial that any of the problems identified by the professionals exist ... External pressure by agencies or court, no doubt in part, accounts for the high attendance figures and is often an important initial motivating force". Similarly, Dale et al, (*1986*) in describing their work commented on "The usefulness of the largely unrecognised but therapeutic potential of powerful statutory mandates to engage highly resistant families." Interestingly, the Rochdale NSPCC team found it was possible to rehabilitate approximately 65% of children referred to them back home. Thus there exists positive practical experience in the UK of using statutory intervention, not just for protection purposes but also to assist the change process.

Whilst such programmes may be apparently atypical of general practice, it is important to remember that many other families who are not formally subject to statutory intervention are, nonetheless, often subject to the threat of serious sanctions if they fail to comply with the prescribed action programme. In other words, the use of authority and the threat of compulsion as levers to change, are not so alien to our practice as might first appear. Openness and honesty, and the ability of professional staff to use authority appropriately are an essential basis on which to build a foundation of understanding between parents and professionals.

The issue of power is central to an understanding of child abuse. Its significance applies not just to the relationships between children and their families, but also to the relationships between powerful welfare and criminal justice agencies and families. The ways in which these relationships so often reflect societal inequalities are increasingly being recognised. Feminist theories have shown clearly the need to understand sexual abuse within the context of the unequal distribution of power between men and women in society. Similarly studies of institutional racism have demonstrated the insensitivity and ignorance of white dominated child protection agencies in responding to child abuse among the minority ethnic populations. Underlying both gender and racial inequalities is the fact that the majority of the families in which abuse takes place suffer from socio economic deprivation.

The impact of gender, race and class are thus of major importance in assessing both the causes of abuse and in deciding how to respond. This is even more critical when consideration is being given to the use of a court order with families who already experience considerable powerlessness by virtue of their racial or socio-economic position in society.

For social workers these factors only increase the professional, personal and political dilemmas involved. Stevenson (*1989*) has pointed to the urgent need for "models of interaction between internal and external systems which are meaningful to social workers in contemporary British society, and which relate constructively to feminist perspectives and to the experiences of black families in Britain". Given the deficits in our theoretical knowledge, it is all the more important that as social workers we are clear that children remain the most vulnerable and powerless group in our society.

The relationship between compulsion and change is a complex one, involving both professional and political issues. At its most simple, it is clear that compulsion alone does not lead to change, except in the most concrete and external of ways. The removal of a child from a family creates a change, but only at a first order or circumstantial level. In other words, it is a change of circumstances, which, of itself, does nothing to alter the attitudes and behaviour of parents which put children at risk.

But the converse is also true: compulsion is not necessarily an enemy of change. To understand the relationship between compulsion and change requires a wider exploration of what motivates people to change, and how people change. If this is not understood, then statutory intervention will, at best, produce only superficial and short term change, and at worst, may lead to resentment and scarring, not only for parents, but also for children.

What motivates people to change?

Literature from the non-statutory clinical therapeutic field has traditionally stressed the importance of client motivation. Treacher & Carpenter (*1989*) for instance, suggests that a family must communicate three basic statements concerning their motivation to change.

1. I have a problem regarding the behaviour of myself or another which distresses me.

2. I have tried to solve this problem alone, or with the help of others, and these problem solving attempts have been unsuccessful.

3. I am asking for your help.

Bentovim et al (*1987*) refer to the importance of parents' taking responsibility for the abuse, and for other problems as being essential to their motivation, and an indicator of a hopeful prognosis. However, as one of the studies on court adjudicated treatment showed, external sanctions may play an important and constructive part in creating motivation within in the client to change.

In the child sexual abuse field, the importance of court ordered treatment has been particularly stressed in dealing with sex offenders. Sgroi (*1982*) argues, "The track record in persuading perpetrators of sexual abuse to undergo voluntary therapy, is abysmal ... Perpetrators rarely remain in an effective treatment programme when the pressure to participate slackens ... Why do we ignore the compelling evidence that an authoritative incentive to change his or her behaviour, is absolutely essential for the adult perpetrator of sexual abuse." One of the reasons why we ignore such compelling evidence is to do with traditional therapeutic beliefs and principles that "to require a client to undergo therapy against his will, almost guarantees therapeutic failure". Motivation comes from an interplay of internal and external factors, and it is rarely the case that real change is accomplished only on the basis of personal motivation without the assistance of external reinforcement.

In the child protection field we need to work with both external and internal motivators. We are involved in care and control, protection and treatment. Clarity about the source of motivation is crucial to effective treatment work. One of the most common pitfalls is misjudgment of clients' motivation and commitment to change. In our work with abusing parents it is not always easy to distinguish between compliance and change. The Children Act will underline the importance of accurate assessment of motivation. In arguing for a statutory order we will need to demonstrate in what way the client's own motivation is insufficient.

Internal motivators

"I want to change"
"I don't like things as they are"
"I am asking for your help"
"I have resources to help solve this"
"I think you can help me"
"I think things can get better"
"I have other support which I will use to encourage me"
"I accept that I am doing something wrong"
"I accept what you say needs to change"
"I accept that others are right" (family, friends, community, agencies)
"You defining the problem, clearly helps"
"I understand what change will involve"
"I accept that if I do not change, you will take my child away"
"I can change if you do this for me"
"I'll do whatever you say"
"I agree to do this to get my child home"
"It's your job to solve my problem"
"You are my problem"
"I am right, you are wrong"
"I do not have any problems"

External motivators

figure 1

We can consider motivation as existing along a continuum and this can help us assess the level of motivation. (*See figure 1.*)

Motivation continuum

Clearly the greater the client's own motivation for appropriate change, the less likely it will be that a court order is necessary.

How do people change?

Protchaska & DiClemente (*1986*), reviewing 18 major therapies, sought to draw out the core components of the change process. From this, they produced "A comprehensive model of change". This model is particularly relevant to working with child abuse. (*See figure 2 opposite.*)

Pre Contemplation

At this stage, many families are at the point where agencies are deciding how to respond to an incident of abuse, ie, significant harm has already occurred. Families are often defensive and reluctant to look at the real issues. The motivation for change is often far greater in the agencies than in the family. Assessing the family's ability to move to the contemplation and action stages will be an important factor in judging whether there is a need for a court order.

Contemplation

Assisting families with deeply entrenched patterns of dysfunctional behaviour to make a serious commitment to change requires considerable skill, patience and effort. The crisis ridden nature of some families means that one is often dealing with a moving target. Simply gaining sufficient stability to assess and catalyse the family's motivation can require the use of statutory invention. This may in itself act as a powerful external message that things must change. The clearer the family is as to what needs to change and why, and the costs and benefits of change, the better the chance that it will stay in treatment. For some families a court order will be a necessary external sanction to reduce the chance of drop out.

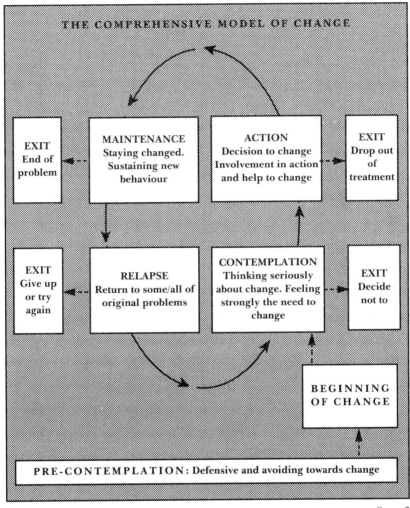

THE COMPREHENSIVE MODEL OF CHANGE

| EXIT
End of
problem | MAINTENANCE
Staying changed.
Sustaining new
behaviour | ACTION
Decision to change
Involvement in action
and help to change | EXIT
Drop out
of
treatment |

| EXIT
Give up
or try
again | RELAPSE
Return to some/all of
original problems | CONTEMPLATION
Thinking seriously
about change. Feeling
strongly the need to
change | EXIT
Decide
not to |

BEGINNING
OF CHANGE

PRE-CONTEMPLATION: Defensive and avoiding towards change

figure 2

Action

Research on treatment has shown the importance of targeting specific treatments for specific problems, and in an ordered sequence where there are multiple issues. Treatment is also much more effective where concrete and visible outcomes are agreed. Thus in contrast to the Contemplation stage, with work on self-evaluation, general ventilation of

95

feelings and on specifying problems, this stage will be more action oriented. Examples might include behaviourial work on child management problems or marital work.

Maintenance

By this stage the emphasis is on the consolidation of changes. The family needs to know and accept the dangers of problems re-emerging, and be willing to seek help to prevent relapse. Stability and support will be essential to sustaining change, especially with the many families who have such poor experience of problem-solving.

Relapse

This cyclical model of change allows for the reality that few people succeed first time round. Change comes from repeated efforts, re-evaluation, renewing of commitment, and incremental success. Relapse is thus part of, rather than necessarily hostile to, change. Change is a battle between the powerful forces that want us to stay the same, and our wish to be different. Court orders in some cases will be crucial in monitoring plans to protect the child. The eclectic nature of this model is its greatest asset however. Different types of treatment and services will be relevant at different points of the change cycle. Few cases will be resolved simply through a single treatment. The task is to coordinate different interventions to ensure that they do not become mutually disqualifying, especially when attempts are made to integrate care and control.

When and how should statutory intervention be used?

Whatever efforts and resources are directed towards voluntary partnership with parents there will always be a significant proportion of abused children for whom a level of intervention involving court orders will be necessary. But authorities must be clear what rights an order will give them, and how this will assist the process of change.

The making of either a care or supervision order can only follow the court finding that the child is suffering, or is likely to suffer, significant harm attributable to the care given or not given by his or her parents.

Both orders can thus have a powerful therapeutic effect in making clear that the care of the child has been unacceptable, and that the parents must take steps to improve their care. This, in itself, can be a first step in the family re-evaluating itself and 'contemplating' seriously the need to change.

Beyond this, the effects of care and supervision orders vary considerably. A supervision order will still only require the supervisor to advise, assist and befriend the child, and take such steps as are reasonably necessary to give effect to the order. These steps are not specified. A new feature of the Act, however, enables courts to add a direction to a supervision order, in relation to a responsible person, such as a parent. The direction, to which the responsible person must consent, will encourage behaviour or actions which should support the purpose of the Supervision Order. In theory, such a power of direction might be used to obtain the involvement of parents in, for instance, family treatment sessions although this remains to be tested. A court may include directions for medical or psychiatric assessment and treatment in a supervision order. A supervision order may also be accompanied by the making of another Section 8 Order, such as a residence order.

Unless the direction to the 'responsible person' carries some clear sanction as to the consequences of non-compliance with the supervisor, supervision orders are likely to remain very limited as a statutory instrument for overcoming the resistance of 'pre-contemplating' parents to entering a treatment programme. Henry Kempe (*1985*) said "You cannot protect a child at home, if he is not safe, by casework". Where the treatment of someone within the home is integral to the on-going protection of a child within that environment the degree of compulsion required of that person to enter treatment must be carefully considered. Inter agency approaches may encourage the use of orders within the criminal justice system in appropriate cases.

A combination of orders available under the Act would make it possible to:

• Separate the child from the parent

• Determine where the child shall live

- Prevent the removal of the child from a determined residence

- Control the child's contact

- Exercise control over the extent to which parents meet their parental responsibility

- Require parents to be involved in treatment

- Provide medical treatment with the child's consent, if applicable

- Establish and require certain standards of parental care

When a care order is made, although both the local authority and the parents will share parental responsibility, the local authority will have extensive duties and powers to plan for children. The court will need to have been satisfied that it is better for the authority to have these powers than not. Local authorities will have to decide whether they can demonstrate that circumstances exist which would make a care order of greater benefit to a child than the use of other orders, for example Section 8 orders, ouster orders or exclusion orders, which may have already been made. Cases in which a care order should be sought will always be difficult. Nevertheless, the following factors should be considered in making a decision:

1. Severity of abuse, eg sadistic, failure to thrive, life threatening

2. Cause of abuse

3. Prognosis for sustained change

4. Motivation for change

5. Availability of treatment resources

6. Parents deny or seriously minimise the presence of other serious problems, such as drink or drug abuse

7. Where parents have dropped out of or failed to engage with previous voluntary treatment programmes

8. The likelihood of re-abuse is very high

9. Parents have very little empathy or bonding with the child, or seriously blame or scapegoat

10. The parents have an assessed limited capacity for change

11. Where children are fearful or request own protection

12. Whether alternative legal arrangements need to be made, eg someone else needs to acquire parental responsibility.

Conclusion

The Children Act will demand that authorities offer greater clarity about the criteria for statutory intervention and to ensure that the appropriate multidisciplinary contributions have been made to the assessment of significant harm and its consequences. Equally, there will be a need to be clearer about the circumstances in which an order may be necessary in the process of achieving change. In arguing for statutory intervention authorities will need to be much clearer about how people change. Drawing together what we know about change and treatability, four criteria can be highlighted as important when assessing the need for statutory intervention:

- severity of abuse

- motivation

- prognosis for change

- availability of treatment

The use of compulsion should be kept under constant review and a switch made to voluntary working wherever appropriate and consistent with the child's protection. Courts and local authorities will, throughout, need to hold a careful balance between the preferred alternative of working on a voluntary basis and ensuring the protection of children.

Bibliography

Asen, George, E., Piper, R., Stevens, A. (1989). A systems approach to child abuse. *Child Abuse & Neglect* **Vol 13 No 1**: 45–58.

Bainham, A. (1990). *Children: the New Law.* Family Law.

Bentovim, A., Elton, E., Tranter, M. (1987). Prognosis for rehabilitation after abuse. *Adoption & Fostering* **Vol 11 No 1**: 26–31

Bentovim, A., Boston, P. and Val Elburg, A. (1987). Child sexual abuse – children and families referred to a treatment project and the effects of intervention. *British Medical Journal* **Vol 295**: 1453–1457.

Cohn, A., Darro, D. (1987). Is treatment too late? What ten years of evaluative research tells us. *Child Abuse & Neglect* **Vol 11**: 433–422.

Dale, P., Davies, M., Morrison, T., Waters, J. (1986). *Dangerous Families*. Tavistock.

Department of Health. (1990). *An Introduction to the Children Act 1989*. HMSO.

Dubowitz, H. (1990). Costs and effectiveness of interventions in child maltreatment. *Child Abuse & Neglect* **Vol 14 No 2**: 177–186

Eekelaar, J., Dingwall, R. (1990). *Reform of Child Care Law: practical guide to the Children Act 1989*. Routledge.

Famularo, R., Kinscherff, R., Bunschaft, D., Spvak, Fenton, T. (1989). Parental compliance to Court ordered treatment interventions in cases of child maltreatment. *Child Abuse & Neglect* **Vol 13 No 4**: 507–514.

Jones, D. (1987). The untreatable family. *Child Abuse & Neglect* **Vol 11**: 409–420.

Kempe, H. (1985). In *A Child in Trust*. London Borough of Brent and Brent Health Authority.

Kolko, D. (1987). Treatment of child sexual abuse; programme progress and prospects. *Journal of Family Violence* **Vol 2 No 4**: 303–318.

Miller, A. (1983). *For Your Own Good*. London: Faber & Faber.

Protchaska, J., Di Clemente, C., (1986). *Towards a Comprehensive Model of Change in Treating Addictive Behaviours, Processes of Change*. R. Miller and N. Heather (Eds.). Plenum Press.

Sgroi, S. (1982). *Handbook of Clinical Intervention in Child Sexual Abuse*. Lexington Books.

Stevenson, O. (1989). *Public Policy and Professional Practice*. Harvester and Wheatsheaf, p 172.

Treacher, A., Carpentar, J. (1989). *Problems and Solutions in Family and Marital Therapy*.

White, R., Carr, P., Lowe, N. (1990). *A Guide to The Children Act*. Butterworths.

Wolfe, D., Aragona, J., Kaufman, K., Sandler, J. (1980). The importance of adjudication in the treatment of child abusers. *Child Abuse & Neglect* **Vol 4**: 127–175.

Cultural and ethnic perspectives on significant harm: its assessment and treatment

Annie Lau

The Children Act places a requirement to work in partnership with the families of children towards whom a service is being proposed, whether this service is one of assessment of need, of significant harm, of treatability, or of provision of alternative accommodation. The 'partnership' requirement applies regardless of whether the arrangement is voluntary, as in a Special Needs assessment, or involuntary, as would follow a Care Order. The concept of partnership implies that one so informs oneself that one can take the views of parents into account in making plans for the child. This is difficult enough in the adversarial context in which child care proceedings normally take place; it becomes doubly difficult when one is dealing with an ethnic minority family.

In this paper I shall attempt to address some relevant issues which may serve as practice guidelines. I am of Chinese ethnic origin and come from a traditional, hierarchical Singapore Chinese family. My early professional training was in Canada, and since 1979 I have worked in the UK as a Consultant in Child and Adolescent Psychiatry. The case examples used in this paper reflect my current practice.

When one is called out in an emergency to investigate an allegation of abuse, what does one need to think about? What is the worker's previous experience of working with ethnic minorities – is this 'coloured' by frustration and a sense of failure? How does one join or engage with these families, explore sources of strength and competence, look at the social and family context in which the alleged difficulties in individual or group functioning have given rise to professional concern?

Sources of strength, individual and family competence, are often to be found in the ethnocultural roots and traditions of the group. Religious belief, for example, often provides a source of important cognitive orienting concepts by which the individual or group structures value systems, role relationships and expectations within the family. These belief systems and value orientations also provide a framework in which crises in life- cycle transitions can be successfully managed. Similarly, extended family traditions with 'old fashioned' concepts of family honour, filial piety (where loyalties to parents take precedence over all other loyalties), and 'reciprocal obligations' which ensure an enduring network of kinship loyalties have in many traditional, hierarchical, families proved to be indispensable in ensuring family survival. However, conflict between traditional family values and those of more egalitarian, nuclear family structures may generate unbearable family tensions leading to family breakup, loss of morale and self-esteem, and abuse inflicted on more vulnerable members of the family.

In order to be able to assess abuse and the presence of Significant Harm in the different societal contexts found in the diverse racial and ethnic groups in the UK, one needs an appreciation of the range of this diversity, and the variations within ethnic groupings from traditional to modern/egalitarian. The author suggests it is important to start out with an understanding of one's own ethnocultural roots and value systems. The worker from a family background with an egalitarian role model, and non-hierarchical relationships among the siblings as a valued norm, may find it difficult to work in a context where the father is the 'head of the household', as will be found in the majority of Asian and Vietnamese families; also special rights and responsibilities are conferred onto older siblings, especially the eldest son. Similarly it would be difficult not to over-identify with the marginal adolescent who feels the only way she could protest against family expectations of an impending arranged marriage is by taking an overdose. It may be for the worker that the very idea of an arranged marriage is itself so odious that he/she forgets to explore other factors in family functioning where deficiencies may have led to the present crisis, for example, failure of mechanisms for conflict resolution and tension diffusion, or the presence of other serious problems like parental alcoholism or the existence of gambling debts.

The worker needs to be able to maintain a stance of professional neutrality, in order to facilitate and mobilise the family's capacity to make choices instead of making decisions for them. Unfortunately his/her normative assumptions about personhood in a family may be interfering significantly with the need to be neutral. Also, in order to mobilize strengths based on ethnocultural roots, one needs to know what these strengths are before one can devise a strategy to mobilize them.

How then does one learn about these differences? Can and should one 'find out from the client'? In an emergency assessment situation one is under a great deal of pressure to make judgements. It is however important to realize we all make judgements on the basis of what we think intuitively is right. The difficulty comes about when these 'intuitive judgements' are based on ethnoculturally defined values. This is compounded when the worker's only experience of particular ethnic groups is in the grossly abnormal context of an assessment under the Children Act. One then cannot depend on these highly disadvantaged and stressed clients, who may or may not be behaving in a deviant manner, to teach you about cultural values in their own community. One needs previous experiences with normally functioning members of that ethnic community, where one can see the cultural assumptions and practices with which one disagrees, operating within the life of that community.

In the spirit of true partnership, it would be helpful for the local authorities to discuss the question of significant harm and procedures for investigation and assessment with community representatives of the main ethnic minority groups in their areas. This may involve religious organisations or community associations and will enable valuable links to be established before crises occur. Aspects of communication, for example link workers, can then be addressed and community views ascertained, while misunderstandings can be clarified. Local authorities can then operate in a context in which they feel supported by elders from ethnic communities.

From a practical perspective I would suggest that the following findings would require immediate steps towards a thorough investigation, whether or not the worker was familiar with ethnocultural issues that may have a bearing on the case:

- the presence of actual physical injury;

- discrepancy between the child's account of events leading to the injury and the explanation offered by parents or caretakers;

- corroborative evidence from another agency with considerable opportunity to observe and report on the child's status, eg school nursery or day centre.

The following areas pose common dilemmas in the assessment of significant harm with regard to ethnic families:

- family structures that do not conform to Western European norms

- 'culture bound' symptoms

- culture-determined child-rearing practices

Family structures that do not conform to Western European norms

1. Single parent Afro-Caribbean families

Despite the rise in single parent families in the UK, the white one-parent family is still widely regarded as deviant from the Western European ideal. In the same way, society still views the family structure of single-parent Afro-caribbean families as deviant. Studies of working-class family structure in the West Indies, for example Henriques (1949), clearly show the stability of the matricentral family grouping, around a consanguineous basis rather than a conjugal basis. Extended family links are often built around mother's blood relationships and a strong sense of kinship extends beyond the immediate mother-child unit, in working class families. Also, long established links albeit 'informal', as for example Godparents or Grandfather's long standing co-habitee, may be invested with the same degree of authority and influence in family matters as the biological Grandparent in a traditional Asian family. Thus for the single parent Black mother her links with her mother and brothers are extremely important. In father's absence, maternal uncle was often the most important authority figure in a young Black boy's upbringing.

2. Extended family groupings in the same household

The assessment and management of intergenerational conflict in the same household is often a difficult one for therapists from a Western European nuclear family structure. One needs to know what authority structure exists, and what rules govern role relationships and expectations of behaviour; and how the presenting problem is linked to the rules and beliefs.

Case example: An infant was admitted to a paediatric ward with a second head injury in 6 months. The mother admitted responsibility for both accidents, and said on the first occasion the child had fallen out of her rocker while rocking vigorously, and on the second she had been careless and the pushchair had slipped down the stairs with the child still in it while she was busy unloading the shopping. Paediatric staff reported the mother to be warm and attentive towards the baby in hospital, and appropriately involved in her care. We felt, however, that something was not quite right.

I asked to see the family, from a traditional Sikh background. They were initially unwilling to disclose 'private' family matters until I pointed out that their family honour could be involved. It then emerged that the mother was in an extremely vulnerable situation. This was a family where she was the only daughter in law to have come from Kenya, whereas the others were all British born. Being less conversant with British ways, she had accepted the role of being the family childminder for all the pre-school children in the family while the other women went out to work. In the mornings therefore she had been overwhelmed with the pressures of providing childcare to four children including her own baby, and was also expected to do the shopping. Out of a sense of pride, and the need to prove her 'worth' to the family, she had not complained or asked for help from her sisters in law. A steep flight of stairs led directly to a narrow kitchen, and she had been putting the groceries away when her four year old nephew pushed the push-chair down the stairs. To complain about the behaviour of a senior sister-in-law's son would have been difficult, and challenged the hierarchy in the female network.

This family was helped to move from a position in which the young wife was being asked for a solution she could not give, to one in which the family could accept collective responsibility for protecting her and the children. The strategy was one of mobilizing family strengths through invoking the concept of family honour. Thus the therapist respected and accepted the authority structure of the family and its rules, one of the most important of which was the principle of inter-dependence.

Culture bound symptoms

Ethnic minority clients may present with maladaptive behaviour and symptoms influenced by the religious and symbolic language of the culture of origin. This may include a preoccupation with ghosts in incomplete mourning (*Henriques, 1951*); or spirit possession in conservative Muslim families or Chinese families from a rural background, often activated in a context of insoluble family conflict. Even though the symptoms and behavioral patterns may not fit established patterns of deviance in the wider British context, still the cultural patterning would be familiar to her members of the same ethno-cultural group and may not be seen therefore as irrational and inexplicable. The symptoms and behavioral patterns may conform to cultural expectations of how one gains entry to the sick role. For example in Chinese communities depressed patients most commonly present with somatic complaints, and in the Chinese language depressed affects are couched with reference to the body.

Transient psychotic states in which the long term prognosis is usually good, is also found more commonly by psychiatrist in patients from an ethnic minority background. This needs to be taken on board in the assessment of future parenting capacity.

Case example: An Afro-Caribbean mother was felt by attending medical staff to have made a good recovery from a stress induced psychotic state. She was still however anxious about her housing condition and despite support from Environmental officers, had not been re-housed. While in a psychotic state her symptoms had a marked sexual content. Her social worker refused to support her request to have her children removed from the At Risk register on the grounds that she was still abnormally preoccupied with sexual matters and the children were therefore still at risk.

As a consultant to the system I was told by the social worker that on recent home visits the mother would talk incessantly about 'cocks' and ask for help to get rid of them. She would also be abnormally concerned about the state of her children's bottoms. The social worker was white and said the relationship with the mother was not a comfortable one, she was hard to understand.

I interviewed the mother on her own initially. There were no signs of mental illness. She had however a strong Afro-Caribbean accent. She said she had seen her social worker recently and on each occasion had tried hard to tell her there were cockroaches all over the place especially in the summer heat and could not understand why she did not take her seriously.

I also saw her with her children, aged 3 and 5. At one point they had to go to the toilet and I encouraged them to go by themselves. After they had left the room the mother said she usually had to make sure they cleaned their bottoms properly. On the children's return I inspected the bottoms. Neither child had wiped her bottom properly; the anuses were red and faecal matter was still present.

This was a case in which the social worker's professional neutrality had been compromised by communication and relationship difficulties with the client. It also included a lack of understanding of the nature of transient psychoses. The social worker had been accused of being racist, which made her even more defensive.

Culture determined child-rearing practices

Given the importance of inter-dependence and family connectedness across the generations as a goal for the socialization of the young, it should not be surprising that patterns of child-rearing in traditional extended families would be different. The child from a traditional Asian or Vietnamese family may be sleeping with mother or grandmother for many years; indeed co-sleeping arrangements are often preferred in these families even though there may be adequate space for individual bedrooms. As the child grows up, he/she will have frequent and regular contact with members of the extended family. Through regular participation in family rituals such as meals, outings, festivals, religious events, the child learns his/her place in the kinship system and the rules governing relationships, and expected behaviour. Thus an older sibling will learn to take responsibility for a younger sibling; or to contribute to the family welfare by helping in the shop on the weekends. It will be a source of pride to 'so behave that your parents will be proud of you'. The young person learns the importance of maintaining the honour of the family by his or her public actions. Within the family boundary, he/she will also learn the importance of manoeuvres for diffusing tension in the family. Discipline is usually strict; the family cannot afford to lose face in the community. A fuller discussion of the differences in family developmental tasks in traditional extended families is to be found in 'Psychological problems in adolescents from ethnic minorities' (*Lau, 1990*).

Refugee families

Families with a refugee background will need to be handled with particular understanding for the traumatic stresses which have been part of the family's recent experience. Adults will to a varying extent carry features of Post Traumatic Stress Disorder. For many, the stress of not being able to communicate in English will be extremely disabling, particularly for recent arrivals to this country.

Case Example: Two boys aged 6 and 9 were referred to a Child Guidance Clinic by the school with concerns for their 'cruel and sadistic' behaviour, which included pushing other children down the stairs. They had arrived in the borough some two months ago, speaking no English. The family were political refugees from a Francophone African country. Both parents had been victims of torture and mother bore obvious scars on her arms. The Clinic team met with the mother in her home with an interpreter. She said her husband was still in the country of origin and in prison. The boys did not know their father was missing and were told he was away on business. The mother described the boys as well-behaved at home and not a source of concern. We noted there were several letters offering health checks for the baby of about 6 months that had not been responded to. The mother spoke no English and did not know anyone who could translate or interpret for her.

Several follow-up sessions were then unattended without notice. On one occasion we arrived at the house to find the children had been left in the care of the oldest child aged 10, who did not know where mother was. The children seemed calm and settled, however, including the baby. On a subsequent home visit we found father, who had just arrived in the country after being smuggled out. He felt the need to be wary; there were likely to be death squads after him given his political status back home. He had clear symptoms of Post Traumatic Stress Disorder, with recurring nightmares and somatic symptoms. When informed about the school's concerns his first response was to be angry and he threatened the school with litigation. At the same time the school was frustrated with the lack of resources available to help them with the children's language needs.

These refugee parents were particularly vulnerable on account of their refugee status and past experiences of overwhelming trauma and loss. These experiences, and distrust of bureaucracy, affected their capacity to negotiate with the school. Father's unreasonably threatening attitude at the school obviously reflected the violence of his recent past, as well as the family's bewilderment at the uncertain present. Mother also could not understand our worry about the 'children being left alone'. The missed sessions had to do with necessary trips to the Home Office which she had to keep secret as the discussions were about her husband. Also the children were left in the care of the eldest child who she felt was adequate to the task. The children's behavioral disturbances were understandable in terms of their confusion at not knowing what was happening to their father, and at the same time realising something was upsetting to mother but could not be talked about.

Placement issues

Given the massive over-representation of Afro-Caribbean and mixed race children in care, discussion on placement issues of ethnic minority children has largely focused on the special needs of this group. There is currently considerable debate on the same race versus transracial placement issue, relevant to adoption and fostering. Tizard has questioned whether even the concept of a 'positive racial identity' is a valid entity, as current research has failed to demonstrate links with self-esteem. The

Children Act however clearly says race, language, religion and culture need to be taken on board in placement considerations.

Case example: The adoptive parents of a 10 year old boy of mixed race origins (White-Afro-Caribbean) complained of his 'attitude' problems. He would come home from school in a bad mood and get into an argument invariably with his father. Both adoptive parents were white, as was the other adopted child from infancy, a girl. Eventually on direct exploration he said it would be easier for him in his family if he were White, because he would not be called 'Nigger' by both his cousin and the boys in his school. He felt his parents did nothing about the racist abuse both within the family and outside it. The parents had told him it was 'just name calling' and he had to learn to put up with it and not get into fights. I noticed that I had to draw attention to the racist aspects of what the parents referred to as 'name-calling' as they were anxious to minimize the racial differences between them. In fact it became apparent that racial differences were not discussed. In time however it felt safer to do so and the parents appreciated their son's particular needs for support for his racial identity within the family as well as the school. This led to a considerable improvement in the relationship between the boy and his father.

Case example: An adolescent girl of mixed UK White-Hong Kong Chinese parentage was placed in care following allegations of abuse. The girl was classified as Black, assigned a black social worker and placed with a Black family. In this case, the social worker as well as the foster family turned out to be Afro-Caribbean. The girl's Chinese father found it difficult to think of his daughter living, as he put it, with 'Black devils'. Issues of ethnicity and language had not been explored directly with the girl who had been exhibiting extremely disturbed behaviour, including wrist-cutting and repeated suicidal threats, as it was felt by professionals involved this may precipitate further disturbance.

As a consultant to the network, I was allowed to interview the girl after I reported my separate interviews with the parents elicited the information that she had been a fluent Chinese speaker. In fact the mother had been enraged by the conversations between this girl and her father in Chinese as it excluded her. I interviewed the girl in Chinese and it was clear she could understand what I said, though she was hesitant to reply in Chinese as she did not feel she could be sufficiently fluent. She said it was the first time for over a year that she had heard the language which she associated with the happiest period in her life, her early childhood spent with grandparents and extended family in Hong Kong. She showed me that she could still write her name and a few characters in Chinese. Over the past year no provision had been made to help her maintain links with the Chinese community, or to support her use of the Chinese language. She wanted to be able to read and write Chinese so that she could write to her family in Hong Kong. As they did not speak English, she could not otherwise communicate with them. She said she had not felt able to talk about any of this with either foster parents, social worker or psychiatrist, as they would not understand her wish to maintain a Chinese ethnic identity.

This case illustrates the difficulties in a professional system where the term 'Black' is applied to all ethnic minority groups, and thinking in child care derives solely from the paradigm of the historical conflicts between Whites and Afro-Caribbeans. It meant the child's ethnic identity needs, here tied in closely to positive hopes and aspirations for her future, were not addressed. An important therapeutic potential was therefore not mobilized.

In summary, I have found the following practice guidelines useful in the assessment of an ethnic minority family, and may facilitate the task of 'working in partnership'.

1. What belief systems and value orientations influence role expectations, define and set limits of acceptable behaviour? For example, traditional Islamic views on family life provide for segregation of the sexes, especially after puberty, with the expectation of chaste behaviour for adolescents and virginity on marriage.

2. What are the structures relevant to authority and decision-making in the family? What are the kinship patterns? Which are the key relationships with important supportive functions? What is the relevant family network? Authority structures vary between groups

but in the traditional Asian or Chinese family the concept of head of household is still important and authority may be vested in the most senior male member; often the paternal grandfather. The kinship pattern may be that of the traditional extended family, with the expectation of reciprocal obligations providing the basis of interconnecting family networks.

3. What life-cycle phase is this family at? What are the risks and challenges? What are the traditional solutions used to manage conflict and to what extent are they operational in this family?

4. Where does this family fit in the range from traditional/hierarchical to modern/egalitarian? How is the living unit organised to enable essential tasks to be performed?

5. What traditional networks and activities (based on religious or family ritual) maintained and supported structural relationships in the family? Which of these have been lost, with what consequences?

6. What significant stresses and losses arise from the family's own experience, from the country of origin, from adaptation to the UK? What racial or cultural factors confer advantage or disadvantage to the individual/family in Britain?

For the traditional hierarchical Asian family the authority of the grandparents and a close network of relatives may have maintained a protective and buffering function for its members, enabling conflicts to be worked through before tensions rise to intolerable levels. For other groups the authority of the church, or other religious organisations, may have served similar needs. Immigration to the UK and the loss of these networks may have contributed to increasing helplessness, especially in vulnerable individuals, in an environmental context where new rules are not well understood and communication, particularly language, is poorly established.

A couple from a traditional, hierarchical extended family background who have just undergone an arranged marriage would be in the life cycle phase of early marriage. Unlike their counterparts in the country of origin, they may not have the protection of extended family networks around them. In the author's experience, brides coming to the U.K. to join their husband's family, without ready recourse to their own families of origin, may be particularly vulnerable. It would be crucial for such a bride to form alliances with the network of female in-laws. Her relationship with mother-in law would be especially important in determining her emotional survival in the extended family household, where initially she would be the most junior member in the 'family firm'. This often has implications for the emotional and physical well being of children in the marriage. The reader is referred to 'Psychological Problems in Adolescents from Ethnic Minorities' (*Lau, 1990*) and 'Family Therapy in Ethnic Minorities' (*Lau, 1988*) for a fuller discussion on differences in life cycle issues for ethnic minority families.

Assessment and treatment responses to significant harm must be sensitive to ethnic and cultural issues and enhance the potential for building a working partnership with families and communities. Practitioners should consider two further points to achieve these goals. They should ensure that their clinical hypothesis takes account of the meaning of the symptoms and behaviour presented as deviant for the family, the ethnocultural group and the wider social context, such as the school. They should also propose a strategy for intervention which attempts to mobilize strengths within a context that supports the authority structure of the family and community.

Bibliography

Henriques, F. (1949). West Indian Family Organisation. *The American Journal of Sociology*. Vol 55 part 1: 30–37.

Henriques, F. (1951). *Kinship and Death in Jamaica*. Phylon. Vol 12 part 3: pp 272–278.

Lau, A. (1984). Transcultural issues in family therapy. *Journal of Family Therapy*, **6**, 91–112.

Lau, A. (1986). Family Therapy Across Cultures. In J.L. Cox (Ed.), *Transcultural Psychiatry*. London: Croom Helm: pp 234–252.

Lau, A. (1988). Family Therapy and ethnic minorities. In E. Street and W. Dryden, (Eds.), *Family Therapy in Britain*. London: Open University Press: pp 270–290.

Lau, A. (1990). Psychological problems in adolescents from ethnic minorities. *British Journal of Hospital Medicine*, **Vol 44**, September 1990: 201–205.

Significant harm in context: the child psychiatrist's contribution

David P.H. Jones, Arnon Bentovim, Hamish Cameron,
Eileen Vizard, Stephen Wolkind

This paper has been slightly adapted from a document produced by the authors as a handout and presented at the Judicial Studies Board Series of training events held during 1990–1991, in preparation for the launch of the Children Act 1989.

Introduction

The current practice of child and adolescent psychiatry lends itself well to the needs of practitioners of family law. These explanatory notes set out the approach taken by a consultant child psychiatrist, or child psychiatric team, when examining a child, whether in a clinical or legal context.

As for diagnosis so for treatment, a child's assessment necessarily includes consideration of the parents and other adults concerned. Findings are recounted in the court report, which highlights signs of harm to the child (whether or not attributable to lack of parental care), and signs of emotional and physical neglect, with observations as to cause.

The psychiatric conclusion and recommendations discuss the advantages and disadvantages of various courses of action and concludes by proposing a definitive plan, which will be open to explanation in cross-examination.

This brief introduction to child psychiatry discusses our key concepts and practices, of relevance to court decisions, in relation to the Children Act. The focus of this paper is that element of child psychiatric work which is concerned with child abuse and neglect. The paper considers in turn the developmental perspective, attachment, assessment, diagnosis, formulation and treatment.

1. Development

The developmental perspective emphasises the unfolding of the individual over time, in physical, social and psychological spheres of life. The process consists of a series of basic tasks which, once achieved by the child, remain critical for the individual throughout life. Each critical task may not be so obvious as life unfolds, because new tasks become relatively more prominent. Each sphere of development inter-relates and influences the others. Developmental medicine is concerned with understanding these processes in sickness or in health. This approach also emphasises that a single individual may change dramatically over time in either direction and the developmental approach is to identify key mechanisms with which to understand the individual's development as well as to identify potential influences which might encourage the individual towards health and away from the direction of sickness.

Key tasks of social and emotional development are:

i   The baby's achievement of a balanced state, eg feeding, sleeping and elimination (*During first few weeks of life*)

ii The development of a secure attachment with a caretaker (*During 0–12 months of age*)

iii The development of an independent sense of self (*During 12–30 months*)

iv The establishment of peer relationships (*30 months–7 years*)

v   The integration of attachment independence and peer relationships (*7–12 years*)

(*Age in brackets denotes when the task is most prominent, but the achievement continues to be important to the individual.*)

Not all abused children go on to become damaged children or damaged adults. We tend to see those who do repeat the cycle, but a study of those who do not repeat the cycle has taught us a great deal. For example, the importance of good 'corrective' relationships, success in school, skill, craft, art, physical performance, and the positive benefit of therapy and understanding of the meaning of maltreatment have all been identified as factors which mark out those whose future adjustment is better despite early deprivation and abuse. Thus few single influences on development, including severe abuse, have an inevitable future consequence, and all factors have the potential to affect future outcome in the direction of good or less good states of adjustment. Additionally, the sum as well as direction of such influences may alter over the individual's life course, so that a disturbed child can change, if there is sufficient change in the positive and negative influences bearing on him/her.

The effects of abuse can be observed in all spheres of life. The exact nature of impact will depend upon the stage of development the individual has reached before abuse starts. Effects of abuse are seen in the following areas:

1. Emotional life

2. Behaviour

3. Mental processes (thinking, memorising, language)

4. Relationships with others

5. Physical development

Although effects may be seen in any or all of these domains the most serious impact of severe abuse and neglect crosses boundaries affecting the individual's capacity to form trusting human relationships and his/her sense of self worth and value.

A key element of an individual's social and emotional development is a secure emotional attachment to a parent or caregiver.

2. Attachment

Definition and characteristics: Attachment is a particular form of relationship. Its major characteristics are that it provides a base from which a child can explore the world and that the presence of a person to whom the child is attached reduces the child's anxiety in stressful situations. It lays the foundations for the ability to make lasting relationships and to cope confidently with new situations.

Assessment of attachment: It is assessed by seeing how the presence of attachment figures allows the child to cope with unfamiliar surroundings and with the presence of strangers. The way the child reacts to the departure and return of the parent is an important part of the procedure.

The course of attachment: During the first six months babies begin to distinguish important figures in their life, but any adult, familiar or strange, can usually soothe distress. They can be moved from one care-taker to another with relatively little difficulty. From six to eighteen months infants become increasingly selective. They become upset at attention from strangers and are distressed when their attachment figures leave them. Though the fear of strangers diminishes, the need for attachment to adults remains very obvious until around age three. After this age though attachment remains of great importance, with greater intellectual development, the child can more easily understand why an attachment figure has to leave and will be less distressed by separation.

Breaks in attachment: The loss of the prime attachment figure between the ages six months to three years can be followed by profound distress. If permanent the child can establish new attachments, but often only with great difficulty and much testing behaviour. Multiple breaks can lead to the child being virtually unable to make true relationships. Such children are noticeable by their indiscriminate overfriendliness to adults.

The quality of attachment: Severely abused children can show strong clinging to their parents. Strength of clinging is not a good measure of attachment. The key is the ability of the attachment relationship to pro-vide the two components of increasing confidence and reducing anxiety. Different qualities of attachment can be seen: secure or insecure. With an insecure attachment, the child hardly notices the departure and return of the parent, or alternatively even in his or her presence remains frozen and unable to explore a new environment. Insecure attachment is associ-ated with later problems in relationships. The insecurely attached child may show little distress after a permanent removal though the develop-ment of new attachments may take a long time.

The antecedents of attachment: The term 'attachment' describes a type of relationship between two people. To develop securely it requires contributions from both parent and child. Most children without severe brain damage have the capacity to form attachments. Two factors impair an adult's ability to reciprocate: their own childhood experiences and the quality of relationships they have with others. The parent who received very poor parenting and who has no close relationships with other adults may be very insensitive to the meaning of cues given by their babies and this can lead to an insecure attachment pattern. Parents with a psychiatric disorder which impairs their sensitivity may also have major difficulties. The situation is however never static. Changes in the parents' circumstances can lead to changes in the quality of attachment.

Legal issues and attachment: Knowledge of the course of attachment emphasises the crucial nature of the time in legal disputes. eg removing a child before six months as opposed to waiting until they are one year or older.

This knowledge may need to be applied when suggestions are made about removing a child from an adult with whom it has a secure attachment such as a biological parent who has other difficulties or a short term foster parent who, because of delays, has kept the child throughout the crucial period.

The presence of an insecure attachment may be an important factor when deciding whether parents can meet the needs of a particular child.

3. Assessment

Assessment by child psychiatrists and their teams is usually done through more than one interview. The following factors are considered:

a. The professional network

Information available needs to be assembled, and possible meetings arranged, with health, social work and educational professionals who know the child and family.

b. Assessment of the child

Observations of the child are gathered directly, or indirectly via reports from professionals who know the child. Interviews and observations are tailored to the age, development and cultural context of the child as well as problems raised. The use of drawings, dolls house, play with toys can help children express themselves. With a high index of suspicion of sexual abuse, anatomical dolls may be used to facilitate communication, and reveal traumatic experiences. Observations of intellectual functioning, and observation by members of the team can assist the assessment process.

c. Assessment of the family

Reports and observations of the family may be made, either at home and/or in clinical settings. Tasks, exploration of relationships may be required both for the family together and for particular pairs, with special regard to attachment relationships. Parenting strengths and weaknesses are assessed, together with psychiatric disorders, drug and alcohol abuse, criminal records of violence/indecency, debilitating medical conditions, learning problems and cooperation with professionals. The wider family may need to be explored too, in order to obtain a full picture.

4. The diagnostic system in child psychiatry

The basic task of the child psychiatrist is to diagnose and treat psychiatric disorders in children. Using all available information they will attempt to say whether a child has a disorder and if so what it is and what has caused it. As with all illnesses and disorders child psychiatric conditions are classified in the International Classification of Diseases. For a disorder to be included in this system it has to be demonstrated that there is a consensus amongst clinicians on how to recognise it. In addition, diagnoses should have prognostic and aetiological significance. In child psychiatry a multi-axial system is used with a child being described on five different dimensions. (Diagnoses may be positive or indicate 'no disorder' under any of these headings.)

i. Child's psychiatric disorder

ii Whether the child has specific developmental delays eg reading retardation

iii The child's intellectual level

iv Child's physical or medical condition

v Associated psychosocial difficulties in the child's family or immediate circumstances.

Together these five give an overall picture of the child's needs and vulnerabilities. With any psychiatric disorder the child psychiatrist can comment on possible causes and on the impact the disorder might have on the child's life if different courses of action are followed. With each disorder it is possible to estimate the relative contribution of environmental factors to its origin and maintenance. Different disorders can be placed on a spectrum in which the environmental contribution ranges from almost none to nearly 100%.

Abuse

The occurrence of abuse does not constitute a diagnosis. Abuse may be the outward manifestation, or result, of significant personal and interpersonal problems. Additionally, abuse is often a traumatic occurrence, in itself, for the child and this can lead to psychological consequences. Abuse together with accompanying family dysfunction results in psychological problems for a significant proportion of abused children. Consequently we code both abuse itself and family dysfunction in our diagnostic scheme; abuse under axis 4 and family dysfunction (including parental mental ill health) under axis 5.

Severity of abuse is described separately. The severity is linked to the child's developmental level. Thus a shaking given to an adolescent would have a totally different severity implication from a similar shaking given to a 6 month old baby. Bathing a 15 year old is quite different from bathing a two year old.

5. Formulation and significant harm

The psychiatric formulation is a composite statement about the child, which includes: diagnostic features (described under five headings or axes detailed above), relevant past and present experiences or influences, special developmental, ethnic or cultural needs not fully covered in the diagnostic features, a balanced appraisal of placement needs, taking into consideration parenting strengths and weaknesses, and an assessment of significant harm and the sequelae for the child. The formulation will also present the estimated prognosis for any disorder described and will discuss outcome for the child with and without psychiatric or other professional intervention. The formulation will end with recommendations for the child's best interests, which will cover medical and psychiatric treatment, educational and placement needs. Normally the child psychiatrist will present the formulation within the conclusion section of the court report.

The core placement requirement for all children is that which provides for loving, consistent and protective parents in a secure family home. Ethnic, cultural and religious factors will also be part of the formulation and may affect recommendations for both placement and treatment.

In formulating placement issues for the child, conflicts between 'needs' (of the child for protection, treatment etc.), and 'wants' (of the parents for care/control; of the child for quick resolution of conflict between adults) should be discussed, and a clear statement made about the optimal placement, on the balance of probabilities.

Placement recommendations will be based on the likelihood of lowest significant harm to the child (whether physical, sexual or emotional). Recommendations will usually incorporate the degree of stability in the parents or proposed carers, and their capacity to sustain access contact, the value to the child, and to adults of contact, particularly in cases where the previous abuse is still denied by the visiting parent.

Placement recommendations normally take account of the child's present development needs, bearing in mind the need for prompt action to fit in with the child's sense of time passing rather than adult tolerance of delays. Outcomes for the child, which could occur with and without a change of placement, such as psychiatric disorder, educational difficulties or placement breakdown are highlighted, along with the merits and demerits of psychiatric and other professional interventions. Finally treatment and professional management recommendations are made with follow up arrangements.

6. Treatment

The treatment plan is the concluding section of the formulation. In the plan particular attention is paid to the following: severity of any abuse, the child's state – physical and psychiatric, level of parental care and parental attitude towards abuse or impairment.

Parents' attitudes about the degree of significant harm or impairment range from hopeful, in which parental contributions are acknowledged, to doubtful, there is much less acknowledgement, to hopeless, where there is refusal to acknowledge their own role, or to perceive that any change is necessary.

Treatment begins from the first moment of assessment.

a. During the diagnostic assessment phase there normally needs to be a period of separation to prevent further abuse, and to assess individual and family characteristics and the prognosis for work. The length and type of separation depends on the severity of the abuse, the degree of parenting breakdown, and the attitude towards change. A hospital admission may be necessary to assess a child's potential to grow, a foster home to assess the needs of a severely abused child, and contact with parents to assess both the relationships and potential for change and the degree of authority needed to protect the child and assure appropriate treatment.

b. Work during separation from abuse may require the abuser living separately from the child, or the child living separately from both parents, or the family living in a residential unit. Work will often focus on individuals to resolve traumatic experiences, on understanding and modifying abusive inclinations and on looking at factors from parents' childhood and current finance, housing, need for education, and developing professional-family relationships. Working together between agencies is essential during this phase, using the case conference or legal process to adjust residence, contact, and to monitor progress. Contracts and goals are useful for both families and professionals.

c. Rehabilitation work aims to assess whether the family can live together without intensive involvement of the professional network. Use can be made of family centres, residential units and family therapy, linked with protection and therapeutic work to test the progress made. Alternative child placement must be sought when programmes of rehabilitation prove unworkable. Work may be needed with new family placements to prevent re-enactment of abuse. Contact with the original family depends on assessment of their ability to put the children's needs first.

Conclusion

The child psychiatrist's presentation of information in this way should be of assistance to the Court in selected cases, when deciding whether the child has suffered significant harm. Such information could also aid the decision as to whether such harm is related to parental care of an un-reasonable standard, in relation to the family's cultural context. Further-more, if a determination of significant harm is made by the Court, the psychiatrist's assessment of the likely prognosis will contribute to the Court's decision as to whether or not to make an order, with regard to the welfare of the child.

Significant harm: the paediatric contribution

Margaret Lynch

This paper considers the contribution a paediatrician can make to the definition of significant harm and explores how paediatric evidence can also help the court to decide whether or not all the threshold criteria for the making of a care of supervision order have been satisfied, including whether or not:

1. the child is suffering or is likely to suffer significant harm

2. the harm is attributable to care given or likely to be given to the child

3. the making of an order is better for the child than making no order.

These steps in the court process are compatible with the usual paediatric approach which should produce:

an assessment of the child's condition (diagnosis)

an opinion on the reason or reasons for this including attribution

advice on a management plan (treatment)

the likely prognosis.

Defining significant harm

The definition of significant harm is likely to be the focus of a long term debate, similar to that we continue to experience with the definitions of child abuse and neglect. This parallel makes it helpful to relate the definition of significant harm to the global definition of child abuse and neglect offered by Garbarino and Gilliam (*1980*); "Acts of omission or commission by a parent or guardian that are judged by a mixture of community values and professional expertise to be inappropriate or damaging". Such a definition allows for difference between cultures and, over time, within cultures. It also offers the possibility that the definition of significant harm will similarly change with both shifts in community views and values and increasing professional knowledge. A definition combining community values and professional expertise implies the need for a continuing, constructive dialogue between the community and professionals: something that we have not yet satisfactorily achieved in this country.

In reality when considering individual cases professionals will continue to make value judgements on behalf of society. Often it will not be difficult to decide that significant harm is occurring. As will be discussed in more detail later harm can mean illtreatment or impairment of health or development. Significant is defined in the dictionary as note worthy, having considerable effect or importance. It also implies that some form of external assistance may be needed, at least to the extent of an investigation under s47 of the Children Act. In many cases likely to come before the courts a 'reasonable' neighbour would be clear that a given child was suffering or was likely to suffer significant harm and, further more, that something should be done to stop the harm, for example a child suffering recurrent physical or sexual abuse, a child whose health is obviously being neglected or a child who is left for a long period of time unsupervised. Intervention by professionals in such circumstances is likely to have community backing.

The 'need for intervention' criterion can also aid the paediatrician in her assessment. Where the consequences of illtreatment or impairment of health or development have already, independent of any legal action, resulted in a referral to a paediatrician, there is a good chance that the child has a significant problem requiring treatment ie, has suffered or is suffering significant harm. The way in which the parents subsequently cooperate with treatment proposals may be crucial in deciding whether the child is likely to continue to suffer significant harm as the result of parental care. When the child is to be assessed medically for the first time because of an investigation by a social services department and the concern is impairment of health and development there can be some advantage in initially using local screening services. If this is a child who the GP or clinic doctor would refer on to the paediatric department, child development centre, or other specialist resource, it is likely that this is indeed a child with a significant problem. This approach implies universally high screening services, willing to be involved in child protection and secondary paediatric services that are not resource led. When in the course of a social services investigation an established problem usually warranting referral, for example chronic illness or severe developmental delay, is identified for the first time, it will be important to explore the reasons why the problem had not already come to professional notice. Those parents who have been failed by the system must be distinguished from those who have failed or actively refused to use local child health facilities. It will also be important to explore the extent to which the degree of any developmental delay is agreed as being 'significant'.

Factors influencing the paediatric contribution

The contribution a paediatrician can make to the decision making in an individual case will vary. It will never be more than one piece of a jigsaw puzzle to be assembled with contributions from other professionals and the family itself. Sometimes the piece of the puzzle brought by the paediatrician will be large while in other cases they will have no part to play. It is important for all involved in child protection to be able to consider critically the factors likely to influence paediatric opinion given to courts. Within paediatrics there are numbers of sub-specialities and the areas of expertise will vary between paediatrician. For example not all paediatricians will have been trained in the techniques of developmental assessment. The setting in which the child is seen will also influence the paediatric contribution. When I see a child for half an hour in the outpatients clinic my report is likely to be largely restricted to an assessment of health and physical development. On the other hand if I am able to spend an hour and half in the child development centre, undertaking, often with the help of a speech therapy colleague, a full developmental assessment, my report will be wider and may well include comments on the child's behaviour and interaction with parents.

A paediatrician will also be influenced by additional direct or indirect knowledge that they have of the child. The child may already have been known to the paediatrician or valuable information may be available in past records. A local paediatrician might have treated other children within the family and have previous knowledge of the parents. This information should be shared and may well be valuable in predicting likely outcome for the child. Some paediatricians like myself will find themselves increasingly involved with the second generation of families, being asked to assess children of mothers who themselves were known to us as children. This is clearly a very different position from one where we have just met the family for half an hour in the midst of a busy out-patients' clinic.

In addition to knowledge of the child and his family, our knowledge of the community and the culture from which the child comes is also very relevant. The paediatrician offering an opinion should acknowledge how much she does or does not know about the local community or of the culture from which the child comes. There should be a willingness to seek advice from those close to the culture concerned and we must be prepared to be honest about our own limitations. Paediatricians, like other professionals, will also have their prejudices. This means that sometimes in paediatrics we will find examples of classism, sexism and racism. If it is felt that these or other prejudices are influencing a paediatric opinion, then other professionals must feel empowered to challenge the view being put forward.

Evidence of significant harm

Under the Children Act, significant harm means ill treatment or impairment of health or development. Both illtreatment and impairment are further defined as outlined earlier by White in figure 1 (p.4). In most cases where illtreatment is alleged there will, in addition, be impairment of health and/or development. This may be a consequence of the alleged abuse or neglect, or be the result of more generalised failure in parenting. It is to be hoped that in all cases, evidence of any impairment will be presented and that the outcome of the case will depend on more than proving or disproving the illtreatment. For this to be possible, information on every child's health and development will be needed, together will a willingness to modify the current adversarial approach which encourages, particularly in cases of sexual abuse, court battles focusing solely on the significance or otherwise of a physical sign. Paediatricians will often have contributions to make to the diagnosis of both illtreatment and impairment of health and development. It will continue to be appropriate to call upon paediatricians to comment on evidence of physical ill treatment (abuse and neglect). This is an area in which, over the years, they have become increasingly more confident. They should be familiar with different patterns of inflicted injury, able to detect inconsistencies between history and physical findings and be aware of any possible alternative explanations of physical signs and symptoms. Experience should have made them familiar with the characteristics of the abusing parents' behaviour as well as that of the abused child. When asked to comment on the age of injuries it may be necessary for them to call upon a colleague, for example a paediatric radiologist when aging bony injuries. Paediatricians should also be able to comment on evidence of physical neglect and define for the court what standard of care would be considered to be reasonable for a child of a given age.

The Act gives statutory recognition to the view that sexual abuse is illtreatment. Paediatricians will continue to have a valuable part to play in the assessment of suspected child sexual abuse but the limitations of their contribution and that of other doctors must be respected and understood, both within the professions and by society. Unlike physical abuse, the diagnosis can rarely be made on physical signs alone, while the absence of physical signs certainly does not equate with a false allegation. Furthermore it must be recognised that a medical training does not in itself provide knowledge of the normal and abnormal genital and anal anatomy of children of different ages. Even those of us who have worked with sexually abused children for some years need to acknowledge that we probably still have a lot to learn and are currently unsure of the significance of some physical signs. This means that we will not always be as certain in our opinions as colleagues, parents and courts would like us to be.

Ill treatment also includes abuse that is not physical: this means emotional abuse is included. Although this is traditionally thought of as an area more within the remit of the child psychiatrist, the paediatrician may also, in her contact with child and family, have observed examples of emotionally abusive behaviour. The paediatrician may additionally be able to provide evidence of the consequence of emotional illtreatment on the child's health and development by detailing the impairment that has resulted from the emotional illtreatment.

Paediatricians can appropriately be asked to comment on a child's physical health and development. In their assessment they should define any impairment and suggest the cause or causes. It is often easier to provide an opinion when data is available over a period of time rather than from an isolated encounter, for example the course of a medical illness or patterns of growth. With younger children the developmental paediatrician can also be expected to comment in some detail on wider aspects of the child's development, drawing on their experience of normal child development when judging as to the significance of any impairment. It will often be appropriate to ask for input from other members of a child development team such as the speech therapist, physiotherapist or psychologist. There is, for example, an increasing body of knowledge on the effects of abuse and neglect on language development. For the older child, the teacher is likely to have valuable information on the child's development and progress. Paediatricians, as well as child psychiatrists, may have observations to make on a child's emotional and behavioral state and these should, when available, be included in any report. It is always important to comment on positive aspects of a child's health and developmental as well as highlighting problems. The extent of a developmental problem may only be apparent over time as may the contribution of parental care in its aetiology. Thus, not infrequently, it will be unrealistic to expect one isolated assessment to fully elucidate the extent of an impairment, its cause and prognosis.

In the process of assessing children for possible impairment of health and development it is likely that some children will be found who while not suffering significant harm, will within the terms of the Children Act be 'children in need', that is, unlikely to achieve or maintain reasonable health or development without provision of services under Part III of the Act. The paediatrician as part of her assessment should include recommendations for the services needed to help the child overcome any present impairment or to prevent future harm. An opinion may then be needed from the paediatrician or other professional as to whether the parental attitude makes it likely that the advised intervention can take place without statutory intervention.

Past significant harm

The wording used in the Act allows for present and likely future harm but does not include past significant harm (this does not rule out harm that was occurring at the time emergency protective action was taken but where the hearing for a longer term order takes place later). The importance of past significant harm will be its implications for future significant harm and the paediatrician may well be called upon to use her knowledge and experience to predict the likelihood of future harm in an individual case. This as we know may not relate to the severity of a previous injury. For example a child seriously injured by a depressed mother who has made a recovery and acknowledged her responsibility for the past harm is much less likely to suffer future harm than the child with recurrent minor injuries inflicted by parents who refuse to see any need for their behaviour to change. Data does exist on re-injury rates and on neurological consequences of physical abuse. It would be appropriate to refer to such research when making a case for the likelihood of future impairment of health and development when commenting on both past and present abuse or neglect.

The question of a relationship between past and future harm will also be relevant when considering the welfare of children born to alcohol and drug addicted mothers. Both will have suffered demonstrable harm as the result of abuse *in utero*. However, the likelihood of future additional harm will be related to the continuation or otherwise of the addictive behaviour in the parents.

It must be remembered that past and present significant harm can both result in a child with a permanent handicap and this must then be taken in to account when assessing the child's future needs and the parents' ability to provide appropriate care.

The similar child and reasonable parents

The Act directs that "where the question of whether harm suffered by a child is significant turns on the child's health or development, his health or development shall be compared with what could reasonably be expected of a similar child" (s31(10)). As already indicated, the paediatrician should be able to give an authoritative opinion on what is considered normal healthy growth and development for a child of a given age. This should allow a comparison with the child under consideration to be made. We are, however, likely to see individual variations in the extent to which paediatricians and others will be influenced in their comparison by the culture, social background and living circumstances of families. Carers, including foster parents, can provide valuable observations on a child's development, including how she compares with a similar child. Same race foster placements will help us to learn more of expected development in different ethnic groups, as will discussions on child rearing and child development with natural parents of children seen in general and community paediatric clinics.

It is necessary to be cautious when listing measures developed for children of one culture to assess a child from another. For example, growth charts in routine use were standardised on white children. This does not mean they cannot be used but care must be taken with interpretation. Indeed for any child a report of a single entry on a growth chart is of limited value. A child's height and weight must be put in context and related to parental size, prematurity and physical state. Information about growth monitored over time is of much more value and charts can then be used to plot the pattern for children of all races. The paediatrician should be sensitive to differences in motor development between different races, with the African child beginning to walk much earlier than the White European child. Enquiries should always be made about the languages spoken in the home. Sometimes a child is exposed to more than one, leading to different rates of progress in spoken English. We must also acknowledge that English may itself be used with different structures.

For a child with an illness or chronic handicap not primarily caused by abuse or neglect, comparisons will have to be made with children with similar special needs. Here too we can expect paediatricians to draw on experience gained in their general paediatric practice.

The Act also requires us to make comparisons with the care a reasonable parent would provide for the child in question. Once again, we should expect the paediatrician to help define what this care should be for a child of a given age. For the child with special needs the paediatrician would have to consider the management plan that would be proposed to reasonable parents. The willingness and ability of parents to co-operate with the plan will then have to be explored. When considering prognosis, the expected outcome assuming reasonable parents should be compared with the likely prognosis given the level of care that the actual parents are able or willing to give. The extent of any discrepancy might well influence decisions over the necessity of an order. Children with special needs are often more dependent than children with normal health and development on the ability of their parents to cooperate with professionals. There may therefore be occasions when it will be necessary to make an order on a handicapped child but not on other children within the same family.

Getting the paediatric evidence

Paediatric evidence falls into two areas: diagnosis and recommendation. The evidence is currently available from two main sources: local hospital and community paediatricians and 'second opinion experts'. It is to be hoped that implementation of the Children Act will be taken as an opportunity to encourage input from the first group and to re-appraise the position of the second.

The local paediatrician is likely to become involved in two main ways. Either she will already be seeing a child who then becomes the subject of legal proceedings or the child will be referred because of suspected abuse or neglect for an opinion on injuries or for an assessment of health, growth and development. Such a paediatrician with her local knowledge is well placed to take a global view of the child and family, who may already be well known to herself or her colleagues. She will know something of the community from which the child comes and be able to comment on local facilities available to the family. Currently the potential evidence of such paediatricians is not always given the consideration is deserves. In my experience Guardians ad Litem infrequently request information from the local health services, preferring to commission their own expert who is also unlikely to make contact. Most local general and community paediatricians will attend court, but although they are usually called by the local authority, they see themselves as giving evidence in order to protect the best interests of their patient, the child, and will try to be fair and objective in their opinions. Not surprisingly therefore, they can be distressed by a heavily contested case with 'experts' brought in to discredit their opinions and even themselves, and they may become reluctant to repeat the experience.

While there is a need to ensure better training of general and community paediatricians in court procedures, report writing and presentation of evidence, attention must also be paid to the growing demand for 'second opinion experts'. Not all of these experts are coming from paediatrics and it is worth noting that neither the British legal or medical systems impose conditions or criteria on those doctors who set themselves up as medicolegal experts. It is particularly frustrating for those paediatricians who have for years examined and assessed abused and neglected children as part of their service provisions to see greater credence given to opinions of 'experts' who may well have less direct clinical experience and no responsibility for comparable services.

There are ways in which, with encouragement from legal colleagues, cases can become less adversarial. As has already been pointed out the original examining doctor is unlikely, at least initially, to see herself as partisan. She would be willing to discuss, if given the opportunity, any alternative explanations for her findings. It is also to be hoped that in the future it will be possible to ask a paediatrician acceptable to all parties to undertake examination or assessment. It is to be hoped that those paediatricians best equipped to meet the challenges of the Children Act will be both willing and able to do so.

Bibliography and further reading

Augoustinos, M. (1987). Developmental effects of child abuse: recent findings. *Child Abuse and Neglect* **11**: 15–27.

DHSS. (1988). *Diagnosis of Child Sexual Abuse – Guidance for Doctors*. HMSO.

Garbarino, Gilliam. (1980). *Understanding Abusive Families*. Lexington Books.

Law, J., Conway, J. (1991). *Child Abuse and Neglect: The Effect on Communication Development.* London: AFASIC.

Lynch, M.A., Roberts, J. (1982). *Consequences of Child Abuse.* London: Academic Press.

Royal College of Physicians Report. (1991). *Physical Signs of Sexual Abuse in Children.* London: RCP.

Making professional judgements of significant harm

John Simmonds

"There is something I don't know that I am supposed to know.

I don't know what it is I don't know, and yet I am supposed to know, and I feel I look stupid if I seem both not to know it and not know what it is I don't know.

Therefore I pretend I know it.

This is nerve-racking since I don't know what I must pretend to know.

Therefore I pretend to know everything."

'Knots' R.D. Laing

The judgement of social workers in complex child care cases has increasingly become the judgement on social workers and the conclusion in the public eye is often daming. Mr Justice Douglas Brown in the ruling (*7th March 1991*) on the Rochdale Ritual Abuse Cases said "I regret to say that they (the social workers and others involved) were so obsessed with their own belief of what the children were saying that they resolved to remove these children without any appraisal of the material they had gathered." The way the children were removed, the length of time they were removed for, the lack of contact they had with their parents and the treatment they received in gathering evidence were all criticized. The judge went on to say that the Social Services Department had made a catalogue of mistakes and "serious errors of judgement" which "were not minor, trivial or infrequent breaches but were substantial ones which rendered the information from children valueless and unreliable." The Independent, in a leading article, commented the next day (*8th March*

1991) "When will those responsible – at the local authority, on the judicial bench, and in the Lord Chancellor's Department – resign and hang their heads in shame."

What appears particularly worrying in the reports of this case was the failure by the social workers involved to have followed the recommendations of the Butler Sloss Report (*1987*) or indeed even to have read them. Butler Sloss herself in a comment reported in the Independent (*8th March 1991*) said that the misuse of her recommendations was "almost more than I can bear ... Social workers have said, 'I have read the Cleveland Report and I am faithfully following the recommendations'. Both in that case and those which have gone through my hands, I cannot believe that they have read the report, even the recommendations, because, I have to tell you, they were doing the exact reverse."

These problems could be repeated numerous times in respect of numerous public and internal inquiries where children have died or been abused while in contact with, or even in the legal care of, social work departments. It appears not only that social workers are making substantial errors of judgement in admittedly complex situations but that there is a serious problem in failing to learn from past errors and to follow current guidelines in order to make better judgements in the future.

The Children Act heralds a new era in child care work. Against the background described above, there is clearly much room for improving the decision making and judgement of social workers who intervene in the lives of families, whether to protect the immediate safety of children or to serve their longer term welfare with birth parents or elsewhere. One of the concepts in the new Act that will be crucial to this is that of significant harm (*s.31(2), (9) & (10) Children Act 1989*).

In the future local authorities will have to consider the welfare of children and in decisions to intervene this will be a primarily legal concept. Social workers will therefore need clear notions of what is harmful within the definition of the Act, the extent of its significance and the predictive power of this evidence for the future welfare of the child. This will mean that social workers must master an extensive range of knowledge, skills and techniques about the multi-factorial nature of child development in all its variety. There are complex moral, legal, and psychosocial issues which accompany the delicate balancing act between the responsibilities of parents and the welfare of the child. These must be considered within a multi-disciplinary and multi-organisational context, and responsibility will fall to social services departments to manage and co-ordinate such judgements. These issues have been discussed at length by the Department of Health in 'Working Together' (*1991*) and Protecting Children (*1988*).

Reaching a judgement as to the cut off point – the extent and seriousness of the significant harm – where the parent's refusal or inability to engage in rehabilitative work make alternative family care necessary to secure the child's welfare, will continue to be one of the most critical judgements that any professional person will face in their working life. The demand that professionals develop predictive instruments as a way of coping with the uncertainty and complexity of such situations has had a powerful history – from the flurry of activity that emerged from Sir Keith Joseph's concern that the behaviour of a small number of families was ruining the effectiveness of, then, 25 years of the post war welfare state to the powerful recommendation from Blom Cooper (*1985*) to research the development of predictive techniques.

Judgement and decision making

The response from almost all the child abuse inquiries has called for a mixture of administrative review and increased training. Indeed it was the impetus of the Colwell Inquiry in the mid 1970's that enacted through the then DHSS the largely administrative system of Area Child Protection Committees, Procedural Manuals, Case Conferences and Child Protection Registers that make up the system we have today. Subsequent Inquiries have often focused on the way professionals have adhered to these procedures and agency responses have been concerned, where necessary, to tighten the systems and procedures and ensure their compliance (*Butler Sloss, 1988*). Apart from this, there have frequently been calls for better training particularly in the recognition of signs and symptoms of child abuse and improvement in the understanding of available techniques, frameworks, or theories. Apart from the Inquiries themselves, other research evidence (*Decision Making in Child Care, DHSS, 1985*) has frequently shown social workers to be generally poor in planning and decision making, leading to reactive rather than pro-active work. Other responses have tried to widen the debate by looking at issues from the impact of inadequate resources and heavy caseloads, through to historical and societal issues outside of social work such as violence, discrimination and poverty. While there are many factors that need to be taken into account in understanding social workers and their failures, the one issue that crops up over and over again is that of judgement. Yet despite this being a critical area, it has received very little attention in the literature apart from one paper by Sheldon (*1987*). While therefore it is a central activity whenever an action is contemplated or planned, and will often be the basis on which a social worker might be criticized, it does not appear as a subject in its own right in the knowledge or value base nor is it one of the core skills in the regulations from the new basic training in social work, the Diploma in Social Work (*CCETSW, 1989*). It does however, appear as one of the four elements in the disciplinary framework for consultant medical staff "this concerns a consultant's exercise of clinical judgement in the investigation, diagnosis, treatment and care of patients." (*Butler Sloss LJ, 1988*).

The focus of this paper is primarily to begin discussion on the nature of professional judgement and to explore some of the known problems for professionals in whatever discipline when they make judgements, reach decisions or make plans based on their capacity to make predictions. My concern is to shift the focus from an exclusive concern with 'significant harm' as a clinical/legal entity to include the activity of the decision maker in reaching a judgement.

An exploration of this subject at this point in the implementation of the Act and against the serious doubts in the public eye about the credibility of social workers might seem ill-timed. In order to cope with rapid change, practitioners will be looking for security in order to be able to explore and understand what is new. Easily absorbed formulas, frameworks, guidelines, techniques etc. are understandably welcome as a way of trying to inject some certainty and stability into an environment where everything seems uncertain. What follows therefore may not be immediately welcome or reassuring as it strikes at the heart of professional activity: judgement. While the chapter might be considered most helpful if it were a straightforward guide to making better judgements, it follows a more circuitous route by exposing the complexity of professional judgement. That process necessitates sharing our uncertainties with the public, our clients and other professionals if we are not continually to wound ourselves by claiming or acting with a certainty that we cannot possibly possess.

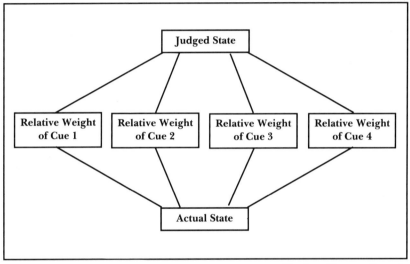

The Lens Diagram figure 1
after Dowie (1988)

The above diagram (*figure 1*) may help clarify this. It is important to be clear that much professional activity (not just in the human sciences) is concerned with the practitioner making inferences from available cues to make a judgement that a certain state of affairs exists. As such the practitioner does not have direct contact with the actual condition but only with its clues or symptoms which are then aggregated in order, for example, to come to the conclusion that a child has been abused. The use of Reflex Anal Dilatation in the diagnosis of sexual abuse is one recent and controversial example (*Hobbs & Wynne, 1987; Butler Sloss, 1988;*

DHSS, Diagnosis of Child Sexual Abuse: Guidance for Doctors, 1988). Professional training is concerned with developing both the knowledge base for and the practical application of such activity. Professional credibility is built on such a framework although it is only rarely that it reaches the public domain with such controversy.

The problem of seeking evidence in order to solve a problem or reach a conclusion can theoretically be done in one of two ways – algorithmically or heuristically. Algorithms involve a systematic search of every possibility until the correct solution is found. We have probably all tried to solve those plastic puzzles found in Christmas crackers that involve sliding numbers or letters inside a square frame so that they run in sequence. If we were to try to solve the problem algorithmically by searching every possible combination, then it might be important to know before you spend any time at all in doing so that there are 20,992,789,888,000 possible arrangements and that at one arrangement per second it will take 663,457 years of your life to complete the task. (*Miller, Galanter and Pribram, 1968*).

Problem solving by such a method is clearly unpractical, which is where heuristics comes in. Heuristics involves solving the problem on the basis of the clues available, and the ability to match these clues to prior experience of these events.

The process of reaching a judgement about situations can be understood therefore as a search for key features in a situation that fit pre-existing ways of making sense of that situation. Searching for somebody that we know in a crowd is not done by looking for them in any whole sense but for the bits of information that fit our perceptual map of them – their gender, height, colouring and so on. Searching for an explanation of a problematical but previously unknown event means perceiving meaning in what to the uninitiated might appear as a random event. Schon (*1983*) says "Problems do not present themselves to the practitioners as givens. They must be constructed from the materials of problematic situations which are puzzling, troubling, and uncertain ... He makes sense of an uncertain situation that initially makes no sense." He says professionals "are coming to recognise that although problem setting is a necessary condition for technical problem solving, it is not itself a technical problem".

While this process is at one level the basis for much professional activity, at another level it is the root of many of the problems in society associated with negative classifications of people and situations – racism and sexism being two of the more powerful. Fundamentally, then, heuristic judgement is the basis of the way that we negotiate the social world in order to survive it. Without our personal and professional maps, the world would be unnavigable. Much professional education and training is concerned with constructing images and maps of the way the world is, or should be, so that the professional person can operate within it.

Sheldon (*1987*) elaborates this using the psychology of perception. He argues that human beings' perceptual apparatus does not simply record the outside world with minimal interference of its own. We actively filter clues on the basis of what should be there and look "scantily to confirm that it is, rather than suspending cognitive processes while we fish for facts (which ones, is the question) and subject these to logical analysis later on." He goes on "We squeeze, alter and redefine discrepant information to bring it into line with previous utterances, rather than radically reappraising our views."

Child abuse poses particular problems in this area because of the difficulty in arriving at agreed operational definitions of concepts like 'significant harm'. Dingwall (*1986*) makes the point clearly "Child abuse and neglect are terms which apply to a particular class of interactions to define them as deviant and worthy of moral outrage ... We may still want to erect standards and to judge other individuals or cultures against them. However, it does direct us to put that exercise in its proper light. Definitions of acceptable and unacceptable behaviour form part of the culture of a society and need to be studied in that context."

Case conferences provide excellent examples of the way that the different cognitive maps that the professions carry around with them can interact (*Hallet & Stevenson, 1980*). How much does the unease often experienced at such events come about through the attempts individuals make to construct explanations of child abusing events that fit their professional and organisational positions and the associated power and status? How far under the pressure of procedural conformity or the need to get to the next appointment can we accept that there are different perspectives on 'reality', reality being as much a function of the positions that we view things from, as our greater or superior ability to perceive reality 'as it really is'? Corby's study (*1987*) of decision making at case conferences found both a lack of identifiable and explicit criteria for assessing the risk to the child and little open discussion about the problems of interpreting evidence, reaching conclusions or planning future action. In his view, the conferences operated on assumed consensus between the participants reinforced by a 'no-conflict' norm. It is not difficult to see the uncomfortable position that any individual might find themselves in if they tried to alter the operating norms of the conference even if their intentions were justifiable in terms of what we know about the complexity of such activity. There may be a related issue here in accommodating to the increasing demands that parents participate in conferences with their different and maybe uncomfortable reality.

The difficulty in matching signs and symptoms to explanations and causes are highly problematic in child abuse and neglect. What is even more complex is the problem of making predictions from the pictures that we construct from the evidence available to us. The whole process is often clouded in dispute, evasion, contradictions and above all uncertainty. Yet at the centre of it is the possibility of a child at risk of its life or at risk of significant harm. The construction of reliable and valid frameworks for guiding social workers and others in their decision making and interventions – for defining and detecting significant harm – is therefore an important and understandable goal.

Two examples of such frameworks were published in the same issue of Adoption and Fostering (*Volume 11.1.1987*). Both articles are forthright in their commitment to the welfare of children and the need for decision makers to be courageous in recognising those parents who have little chance of providing the kind of environment that both protects and facilitates growth and development. They are also full of practical advice and wisdom. In the first, Wolff asks "How do clinicians and specialist social workers make their judgements? What determines their ability to make better predictions than less well trained and less experienced workers?" She goes on to commend three things:

i. accurate recognitions (of signs and symptoms)

ii. a full life history recognising
   a. socio-economic constraints
   b. clinical syndromes

iii. the ability to make a prognosis

She then reviews the research evidence on the significance of depressive illnesses in mothers, her clinical experience of schizophrenia, personality disorder, brain damage and schizoid personality disorders. While she is not explicit about this, the assumption must be that these are the clinical syndromes which need careful assessment and are the bases for making valid and accurate predictive statements and if necessary for "an early disruption of the child's tie to such parents".

In an article in the same issue Bentovim, Elton and Tranter present their scheme for assessing the outcomes of their therapeutic work and the way that they use this to influence their recommendations to social services departments and the courts about the prospects for such work.

Their scheme categorizes families into:

i. those where they predict that rehabilitative work is likely to succeed

ii. those where they have doubts but where there are grounds for optimism

iii. those where there is no hope for rehabilitation.

They detail the characteristics of families in these different categories and in making the assessment look at issues such as:

• who accepts responsibility for the abuse or neglect

• the degree to which responsibility is shared by both parents

• the acknowledgement of children's needs

• acknowledgement of long-standing family problems

- the nature and rigidity of family patterns
- the nature of attachments and patterns of access
- the family's relationship with care professionals

The authors acknowledge that their categorisation is crude and stress the importance of being open to re-defining the prognosis in the course of the work. They also stress the importance of the prognosis being discussed with the family as a basis for identifying success and failure and its consequences.

Jones (*1987*) in an article which compliments the two outlined above also stresses the importance of professionals and public grasping the nettle of the untreatability of some families. In reviewing the re-abuse rates across a number of different programmes, he concludes "More work is needed to clarify the reason or reasons for variations in re-abuse rates (in physical abuse) between different programmes, however it is clear that it is high." (between 16% and 60%). Calling for further research he points to the need for more precise studies to allow us to tease out the relative contributions of different factors to the overall conclusion that a family is untreatable. He identifies a number of significant factors:

- personality variables
- psychiatric diagnosis
- quality of parenting
- family variables
- structure
- emotional tone
- hostility
- communication ability
- capacity for empathy
- involvement of both parents
- type and severity of abuse

- child factors

- completeness of treatment

- therapeutic and professional systems

- quality of substitute care including contact

- process and type of treatment

Further guidance on some of these issues can be found in 'Protecting Children' (*DH, 1988*).

All three of these examples provide the kinds of cognitive maps intended to guide practitioners through the complex and uncertain maze of decision making in child care cases. Given the enormity of the decision permanently to remove children from birth parents and place them in long term foster care or adoption, the development and use of such devices needs to be approached with considerable caution. While they may only be a part of the decision making process and while they may be effective in the hands of experts, their routine use in an organisational context may become more problematic. Indeed the comments of Butler Sloss about the use made of her recommendations cited above is one example of the kinds of difficulties that can arise. To be worthwhile in the longer run they all need the benefit of empirical testing and validation. Although there are a number of errors that can arise in constructing and using such devices, one issue might serve to highlight the difficulties.

There are two potential problems well known to epidemiologists that can arise from any instrument designed to identify and predict potential problems whether they be child abuse victims or other conditions. First, children may be identified as being at risk when they are not: a false positive. Second, children may not be identified as being at risk when they are: a false negative.

Screening instruments can be classified according to two categories

- their sensitivity – the probability that a child who will be abused will be identified as such

- their specificity – the probability that a child who will not be abused will be correctly identified as not being at risk.

While the terms **sensitivity** and **specificity** are usually applied to any formally developed test such as questionnaires, they can also be considered in relation to any method we might use to identify and predict a particular case, even if the method is relatively unstructured. What we would hope for in any instrument that works well is one where we get high specificity and high sensitivity.

The next issue we would need to consider in assessing the performance of the device is the prevalence of the condition in the population as a whole: how often does it occur per so many thousand of the population? The interaction between specificity, sensitivity and prevalence is demonstrated in figure 2.

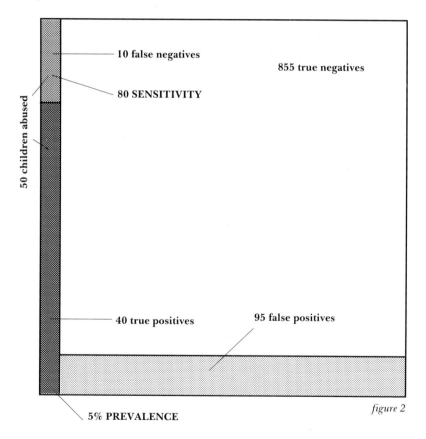

figure 2

If, for example, we take a prevalence rate of 5% ie that 5 children in every 100 will be abused, then in a sample of 1000, we know that 50 children will be abused. If the sensitivity of our screening device is 80%, ie, it is accurate in identifying 8 out of 10 of abused children, then out of our 50 children, we will have identified 40 positively and missed 10, 40 true positive and 10 false negatives. If the specificity of our screening is 90%, then out of the 950 who are not abused, we will have correctly identified 855, and identified 95 as abused when they are not, that is 855 true negative and 95 false positive.

The consequences for the children and families – those who were missed and those who were wrongly identified – as a result of such a hypothetical screening device are clear. The danger to those in the first group of being missed and the injustice, social stigma and waste of resources in the second make the successful development of such screening instruments as a primary preventative measure very unlikely. However, while the statistical problems are real enough, the above example has ignored a major problem that runs through the whole field of child abuse, neglect and significant harm: that of producing a satisfactory operational definition.

Case conferences might be expected to be one of the forums where some of these frameworks are used. However, as Corby (*above*) notes, there is little evidence to suggest that anything as explicit is used as a guide to making decisions. There may be many reasons for this but one that is of significance is the interaction between theoretical complexities of detection, assessment and prediction of significant harm and the organisational context within which such work is carried out. Simon (1947), (see also March and Simon (*1958*), Cyert and March (*1963*), Thompson (*1967*), Galbraith (*1974*), (*1977*)) argues that because of the limited information processing capacity of human beings, organisational members usually resort to decisions based on incomplete information, poor consideration of alternative courses of action and their consequences, and are unable to accurately assess the value of likely outcomes of such action. As a result, human beings settle for quite limited forms of rationality in decision making – what Simon calls 'bounded rationality' and 'satisficing' – decisions that are 'good enough' given the conditions under which they are taken and based on rules of thumb.

Simon develops this theme further by relating it to the ways in which organisations structure themselves by decomposing and routinizing their decision making process in order to make them manageable. The effect of this is for the organisation to develop:

- a set of standard responses to problems

- a way of classifying problems

- rules which determine how the organisation will respond to any given problem.

Much of this is to be found in the procedures adopted by organisations responding to child abuse in their attempts to structure information gathering, processing, decision making and action. While these procedures are intended to be a necessary response to a complex problem, they have an important determining effect on the way an organisation perceives problems, classifies them and takes action in relation to them. They can be seen as the organisation's way of defining, constructing and controlling its reality and not just of responding to it.

While this might be a necessary way for individuals to survive and function at all in a complex world under conditions of often considerable uncertainty, the dangers in the 'satisficing' heuristic are considerable. The routine searching for evidence based on powerful preconceived notions of what we might find and the powerful pressure to make a judgement and act (even if that means doing nothing) without being able to adequately test the evidence, necessarily build error into the system. One might indeed express surprise at the apparent fact that more errors are not made. While the development of frameworks, guides, and screening instruments have undoubtedly made some contribution to clarifying our thinking about child abuse and neglect, the conceptual maps they provide leave out the one significant variable in the whole process – the practitioner as judge. The danger is that they are understood and used as independent of the practitioner who is using them – in my view an important error.

The problem with accuracy in assessment and diagnostic activity is not confined to the field of child abuse and neglect. In 1982 the Working Party on Medical Aspects of Death Certification found significant discrepancies between the reason given for death on the death certificate and that subsequently revealed by autopsy. McGoogan reviewing the results of 1,152 autopsies found that with an autopsy rate of 25%, these was a failure to confirm 39% of the main reason given for death and 66% of the other conditions.

Clinicians certainty of clinical diagnosis	Cases certified clinically	Cases confirmed at autopsy
Fairly certain	47%	75%
Probable	35%	55%
Uncertain	16%	36%
Unspecified	3%	50%

Source: McGoogan (1984)

McGoogan states "... we tried to be conservative and avoid overestimating significance. Nevertheless, we reckoned that more than half the discrepancies were clinically significant in that they might have affected investigation or management."

A number of different methods are available from the decision sciences to help professionals make more consistent decisions. One method does so by modelling mathematically the relationship between the cues available to the clinician and the diagnosis that was subsequently reached. The study of judgement in this kind of way reveals some interesting issues. One of the most important is that what people say they do when coming to a judgement – what they state explicitly to be their method – differs quite markedly from what they actually do when their judgement is modelled mathematically. Dowie (1989) explains "One general conclusion emerging from such comparisons, where they are possible, is that the formula invariably out performs the judge whose policy it captures ... The usual explanation is that since the formula captures the systematic elements in the judge's judging, what's left is by definition 'random', and if we eliminate that 'noise' then he or she will do better. In other words a

151

judge's judging incorporates random error arising out of a variety of 'human' characteristics, such as inconsistency, unreliability and over-confidence."

In one such study, Kirwan (*1988*) modelled the judgement of specialists in rheumatoid arthritis. The results showed a considerable divergence in practice over the relative weights given by clinicians to different presenting features. The effects of feeding this randomness to the doctors concerned had a marked effect in improving their consistency. However, not all such projects have shown positive results. In an analysis of the clinical judgement of physicians of middle ear infection, the researcher was prevented from discussing the results of the study with the practitioners concerned. Chaput de Saintonge (*1985*) reports "I felt that they (the doctors concerned) didn't perceive the benefits that might come out of the study to be worth the risks and losses ... I think most people underestimate the cost of participating in a small group discussion aimed to resolve conflicts of judgement." There may be more resistance to methods that might improve our judgement than maybe we would like to admit.

McGoogan's research is a clear demonstration of the underlying nature of professional judgement – that it is probabilistic and liable to varying degrees of error. A number of other studies (*Goldman, 1983*) on autopsies come to similar conclusions. Although difficult to test, the view in the public mind of the accuracy of clinical judgement is probably very different. Deciding to operate or to administer a particular course of drugs is an all or nothing state of affairs – you take antibiotics or you don't, you have surgery or you don't. However, in reaching a diagnosis and prescribing the treatment, it would probably come as some surprise to hear that for example (using McGoogan's figures), the clinician was fairly certain in only 47% of his decisions and in those he was wrong 1 in 4 times and that this might have made a difference in 50% of those cases. In identifying it as such, the point is not so much that it is so, but that its fallibility is so little in the public domain and publicly recognised. Eddy (*1984*) makes the point clearly, "Whether a physician is defining a disease, making a diagnosis, selecting a procedure, observing outcomes, assessing probabilities, assigning preferences, or putting it altogether, he is walking on very slippery terrain. It is difficult for non physicians, and many physicians, to appreciate how complex these tasks are, how poorly we understand them, and how easy it is for honest people to reach different conclusions". It is difficult for us all to acknowledge that when we make a judgement, that we do so often under conditions of uncertainty.

As we become pre-occupied with mastering the complex technical problems of the Children Act 1989 and look for tools to help us overcome the uncertainty it engenders, it will be important to keep in mind that significant harm is a complex legal, psychological and social concept about which professionals will be making judgements. While there are technical problems to be solved, we must be careful not to respond to the uncertainty about the concept by turning it into a technical professional problem with technical solutions unrelated to the judgement making activities of its practitioners.

Given the ill-structured nature of many of the tasks in child protection and the significant contribution of intuition in reaching decisions, the systems and tools including the organisational arrangements that we develop need openly to reflect and support the uncertain nature of much of what we do. To organise ourselves as though we are conducting a scientific experiment has led us into appearing either over confident in the judgements that we have reached or hopelessly muddled and ill-prepared. We must openly accept and publicly acknowledge that in matters of child care as in most professional activity, the nature of judgement is far more problematic than we have been comfortable in admitting to and the public want to hear. How far can we go on to include our judgement making processes as a key factor requiring as much study and exploration as the children and families we work with? How far are we prepared, as Chaput says, "to accept the cost of participating in small group discussion at the level of practice aimed at resolving our conflicts of judgement"?

The problem with such arguments is that they can lead to a sense of inadequacy and inactivity. It is the case that there are dangerous adults who are capable of killing or seriously injuring, abusing or neglecting their children. The problems outlined above cannot and are not intended to deter us from acting courageously and determinedly. But they should warn us against adopting practices that are inconsistent with the limits of our capacities as human beings, and misleading in their claims of professional judgment. They should also warn us of the risks of adopting defensive strategies and of the importance of developing genuine dialogue with the people to whom we work and are accountable. There can be nothing worse or more dangerous than feeling that you should know what you don't know but that nobody knows it.

Bibliography

Bentovim, A., Elton, A., Tranter, M. (1987). Prognosis for rehabilitation after abuse. *Adoption and Fostering* **Vol 11-1**.

Blom-Cooper. (1985). *A Child in Trust*. L.B. of Brent, p 289.

Butler Sloss, L.J. (1988). *Report of the Inquiry into Child Abuse in Cleveland 1987*. HMSO.

Central Council for Education and Training in Social Work. (1989). *Requirements and Regulations for the Diploma in Social Work*. Paper 30.

Chaput de Saintonge, D.M., Hattersley, L.A. (1985). Antibiotics for otitis media – can we help doctors agree? *Family Practice* **2**: 205–212.

Corby, B. (1987). *Working with Child Abuse*, Open University Press.

Cyert, R., March, J. (1963). *A Behavioral Theory of the Firm*. Prentice Hall.

Department of Health. (1991). *Working Together*. HMSO.

Department of Health. (1988). *Protecting Children. A Guide for Social Workers undertaking a Comprehensive Assessment*. HMSO.

Department of Health and Social Security. (1988). *Diagnosis of Child Sexual Abuse: Guidance for Doctors*. HMSO.

Department of Health and Social Security. (1985). *Decision Making in Child Care*. HMSO.

Dingwall, R. (1989). Predicting child abuse and neglect. In O. Stevenson, *Child Abuse: Public Policy and Professional Practice*. Harvester Wheatsheaf.

Dowie, J., (1989). *Professional Judgement*. Open University Press.

Eddy, D.M. (1984). Variations in physician practice: the role of uncertainty. In Dowie (1988).

Galbraith, J. (1974). Organisational design: an information processing view. *Interfaces* **4**.

Galbraith, J. (1977). *Organisational Design*. Addison-Wesley.

Goldman, L., Sayson, R., Robbins, S. (1983). The value of Autopsy in Three Medical Eras. *New England Journal of Medicine* **308**: 1000–1005.

Hallet, C., Stevenson, O. (1980). *Child Abuse: Aspects of Interprofessional Cooperation*. Allen and Unwin.

Hobbs, C.J., Wynne, J.M. (1987). Child sexual abuse – an increasing rate of diagnosis. *The Lancet* 10th October.

Jones, D. (1987). The untreatable family. *Child Abuse and Neglect* **Vol 11**: 409–420.

Kirwan, J.R., Barnes, C.G., Davies, P.G., Currey, H.L.F. (1988). Analysis of clinical judgement helps to improve agreement in the assessment of rheumatoid arthritis. *Annals of the Rheumatic Diseases* **47**.

March, J.G., Simon, H.A. (1958). *Organisations*. Wiley.

McGoogan, E. (1984). The Autopsy and Clinical Diagnosis. *J. of the Royal College of Physicians of London* **18**: 4.

Medical Aspects of Death Certifications. (1982). A joint report of the Royal College of Physicians and the Royal College of Pathologists. *J. of the Royal College of Physicians of London* **16**: 4.

Miller, G., Galanter, E., Pribram, K. (1960). *Plans and the Structure of Behaviour*. Henry Holt.

Schon, D. (1983). *The Reflective Practitioner: How Professionals Think in Action*. Basic Books.

Sheldon, B. (1987). The psychology of incompetence. In *After Beckford?* Social Policy Papers No 1. Department of Social Policy, Royal Holloway and Bedford New College.

Simon, H.A. (1947). *Administrative Behaviour*. Macmillan.

Thompson, J. (1967). *Organisations in Action*. McGraw Hill.

Wolff, S. (1987). Prediction in child care. *Adoption and Fostering* **Vol 11-1**.